I dedicate this book to all my players, past and present. You have touched my life in so many ways. I will carry our friendships and memories in my heart forever.

A WALDORF APPROACH
TO COACHING TEAM SPORTS

Dean Stark

RSCP

...or the encouragement and support of ... this new edition possible.

*The artist who drew the cover design
can play a little hoop too.*

Cover art: Noah Klocek

Book orders may be made through Rudolf Steiner College Bookstore: Tel. 916-961-8729, FAX 916-961-3032.

Rudolf Steiner College Press
9200 Fair Oaks Boulevard
Fair Oaks, CA 95628

Acknowledgements

Many people contribute to the making of a book. I would like to thank publicly a few special ones:

my mom, Doris Montrose, for her love and guidance.

the Laker family—Dennis, Veronica, Josh, and Andrew—for planting the seed through many conversations to make this book a reality.

David Mitchell and Marianne Alsop of AWSNA Publications who saw the potential of the project and helped steer me in the right direction.

Robin Kraus who spent hours typing both manuscripts.

Judy Blatchford for her wonderful editing of the second edition.

Hallie Bonde for graphic design.

Claude Julien and Rudolf Steiner College Press for their outstanding work in putting this second text together.

Most of all, this book never could have been written without the special relationship I have had with my players, assistants, parents, and colleagues over the years. Thank you all for your support, loyalty, and friendship.

Dean Stark

Author's Note

This entire book is addressed to all coaches, players, parents, and teachers—male and female. I speak from my personal experience which is only with boys' teams. Female coaches and players are making outstanding contributions to the world of sport. I support their efforts and successes. Please understand "she" wherever "he" appears in this book.

Waves volleyball player Beth Dorso demonstrates her classic form.

Table of Contents

Foreword to the First Edition

I remember seeing Dean Stark for the first time in the spring of 1987. He was standing on the white pitcher's mound on the baseball diamond at the Sacramento Waldorf school. Sweep . . . lean . . . throw, sweep . . . lean . . . throw, he was rhythmically pitching to his players. I felt reassured that I made the right decision to teach gymnastics at that school. The same thread of his being ran its course throughout our close working together over the last decade, whether it was a casual conversation about school life, a faculty meeting, or during deeper conversations concerning the guidance of a student in trouble. He listened quietly, at length, and then at last a clarity in his eyes would tell you what he felt, and a wise sentence would be all that was needed.

This is also my experience with him as a teacher, as if he knows that those in his care are on a journey with him for just a short time. His patience is like that of a deep, wide river that moves along without being forced, unhurried—a consistent force, serene and full, carrying the past into the future, while living in the present.

In all of my travels for Movement Education in the Waldorf schools, one of the most commonly asked questions I found concerns competition. It seems the very word "competition" sends vast waves of memories and emotions through the adults that carry these questions. It is because of these questions that I feel honored to write of my knowledge of Dean Stark and to celebrate his courageous steps toward building a much needed bridge to look at the experience, phenomena, and truths of modern sports and competition.

I hope these personal accounts will inspire many more meetings between coach, athlete, parent, and teacher.

Maureen Foley
P.E. Teacher
Sacramento Waldorf School

Foreword to the Second Edition

Just as the human body needs a solid bone system to prevent it from sagging, so does the astral body, with its enclosed I, need ideals at this age if it is to develop in a healthy way. We must take this seriously. Ideals, strong concepts that are permeated with will, these we must impart into the astral body as a firm, solid support.

Rudolf Steiner, *Education for Adolescents*, 1921

If the goal of Waldorf education is to educate the head, hand, and heart, then *A Waldorf Approach to Coaching Team Sports* is highly relevant. It shows how athletics can be a positive part of Waldorf's integrated curriculum, and can also be a wonderful source of pride to an individual school. For those of us in and around the Sacramento Waldorf community, it comes as no surprise that this guide to future coaches and teachers comes from Dean Stark, whose vision and dedication created one of the best—and best respected—athletic programs in the area, all the while remaining true to the principles of Waldorf education.

When Dean arrived at Sacramento Waldorf School, he was in his early twenties and fresh out of college. He no doubt thought it strange that there were more chickens on campus than basketballs, not to mention no baseball fields or indoor basketball courts. Dean was the antithesis of a Waldorf teacher, a hardnosed baseball player with a Schwarzenegger physique who was short on coaching experience but full of confidence and determination. His feet were squarely on the ground. Instantly, he became a student favorite, and slowly, the more traditional faculty began to accept him as well.

By the time I was in eighth grade, the Waldorf basketball and baseball teams were already in the area playoffs, contending against much larger area public schools. High school boys were helping lower school boys learn to shoot basketballs and were becoming role models for them as well. I could see that through Dean, who created competitive teams out of skinny kids who had never played organized sports before, I would be able to go into the Sacramento area proud that I played for Waldorf. The next year, I was a skinny kid proudly wearing an old Waldorf track jersey, playing on a junior varsity basketball team with my friends. We rarely won, but that didn't matter because Dean was our coach, and we were a part of something we all knew was special.

When Dean told us we could be successful at anything if we wanted it badly enough, we knew he was right. In those years, Dean always played with us in practice, and he always played harder than we did. And he always won. When he taught us that the most disciplined wins more often than the physically strongest, we had a hard time believing him until we were able to beat larger schools with strategy rather than strength. We laughed out loud when Dean gave us an impossible task and said, "find a way," and then we quietly began to try to find one. His concepts of motivation, healthy living, and dedication were never confined only to athletes. To non-athletes, as well, Dean brings interest and understanding, and he has been a teacher of valuable lessons that could never have been taught in the classroom.

As much as Dean has changed the Sacramento Waldorf School, the school has also changed him. Some fifteen years after taking that first coaching job, Dean is a class sponsor, a senior member of the faculty in the high school, and a well-respected member of Sacramento's athletic community. He draws upon his study of spatial dynamics to teach physical education and to coach and still smiles knowingly when eurythmy is credited for his teams' coordination and teamwork. He doesn't play on the court in practice with his team as much as he used to, but they still believe him when he says that dedication and hard work are the key to success. He is still teaching boys the life lessons of intensity, perseverance, mental discipline, and physical effort, and when he says "find a way," they still do.

Every year around Christmas time, when Waldorf alumni return to Sacramento for the holidays, we come to Linden Hall, the new gymnasium, for a chance to play in the alumni tournament, and a chance to reminisce with Dean. He had a real impact upon the lives of all of us who were lucky enough to play for him, and he has had a lasting effect upon the way a holistic education is viewed at the Sacramento Waldorf School. Team sports are important in Waldorf schools, and Dean has provided an excellent model of how to integrate them into a Waldorf education and a real reason to try.

Matt Alsop
April 20, 1999

Waves baseball Player Joel Gray delivers another strike.

Introduction

"I haven't played very much, but I've read a lot of books." Those words, which came from a student named Ryan who would turn out to be my best player that season, have stayed with me ever since. The date was February 1, 1984. They came from a student named Ryan who would turn out to be my best player that season and one of my best ever. That season would be the start of something I never could have imagined in my wildest dreams.

As the youngest of four boys, I grew up in a very athletic environment to say the least. I was always trying to keep up with my brothers and thus was always a step ahead of kids my own age. I excelled in all sports but baseball was the one that I was going to make a career in. However, when my playing days were ended prematurely in college because of a serious knee injury, my coaching career began.

The school was called the Sacramento Waldorf School, where my brother Randy was teaching, but otherwise I had never heard of it. The interview went well and I got the job. Even though I was only 21, I really felt that I was ready for the task.

It sounded like a good place for me to start because the school was small and I could gain some valuable experience before I moved on to something bigger and more challenging. My ultimate goal was to coach at the college level.

Nothing, however, could have prepared me for what I saw and heard. First, as I walked down to the baseball field I saw a cow grazing on it. "That's Beverly," commented Dave the high school chairperson. Next, I realized that there were no pitcher's mound, backstop or dugouts.

"We're in the process of improving our diamond," Dave assured me. "Oh, and by the way, league starts in a week and a half."

Later that day, I met with my players for the first time and it was then that Ryan uttered those immortal words about reading a lot of books. It was also then when another player asked me what a base hit was. Right away, I knew I couldn't start any lower than this at any varsity high school in America. I still had time to get out of this. I thought to myself that this environment was so foreign to me. I was used to top-of-the-line facilities, not cow pastures. I was used to talented, experienced athletes, not book readers. But something pulled on me to stay. I felt a sense that they needed me and that I could make a difference in their lives.

Well, it is now twelve years and seven league baseball titles later. I have learned a great many things about coaching and what it takes to make the experience special. I've also learned how to bring competition into the life of a Waldorf school and do it in a healthy and positive way. That's what this book is about.

CHAPTER 1

COMPETITION IN A WALDORF SCHOOL

The credit belongs to the one who strives valiantly; who comes up short again and again; who knows great enthusiasm and great devotion; who spends himself in a worthy cause; and who, at the best knows in the end the triumph of high achievement; and who, at worst, if he fails, at least fails while daring greatly, so that his place shall never be with those timid souls who know neither victory or defeat.

—Theodore Roosevelt

Waves player Dylan Hickey glides down the lane for another two.

In my second year at the Sacramento Waldorf school, I took on the coaching duties of the boys' basketball team. Even though I hadn't had much experience with basketball as a player, and I had no experience as a coach, it was this sport for which the Sacramento Waldorf school became known worldwide as a real power. Wherever and whenever I visited a Waldorf school, people there knew of our basketball team, and in my conversations with these people, two recurring topics kept popping up: first, how did you do it and how can we do it, and second, how does one deal with the dreaded "C" word—competition—which we don't want encouraged here?

I personally think that people who hold the latter feeling have had bad experiences with competitive sports in the past, have never experienced competition brought in a positive way, or are just plain closed-minded and uneducated about the subject.

Rudolf Kischnick, one of the first to apply the principles of Rudolf Steiner's indications for physical education, states in *Games, Gymnastics, Sports in Child Development* that:

> The standard for achievement is the effort. If the pupil does not need to make an effort, he is not conscious of the fact that he has achieved something. In order to let him make the effort one has to set him a goal which has a right proportion to his capabilities. In order to let him develop these capacities, a certain opposition should be put in his way. Exactly in the time between the ninth and eleventh school years the growing human being likes to come to terms with the problems of opposition. For if one does not offer him the opportunity for this now, he will later become undisciplined, when it is important for him to conquer inner oppositions. Also within oneself one has to overcome many obstacles, before one reaches one's value, and not for nothing does destiny give one the opportunity to do, outwardly, during youth, what later one has to bring into practice inwardly.

Brought in the right way, competition can accomplish this. It helps create an avenue for students to be truly passionate about

2

something in their lives. Competition doesn't have to be about winning. I virtually never talk to my players about winning. I always stress playing to their best ability and giving everything that they are capable of. If they do these things and practice correctly, winning will take care of itself.

Being competitive shouldn't mean striving to dominate or overpower an opponent. It should mean that you have set individual and team goals that you are trying to reach. Never make an opponent the means to a goal. If your players walk off the court or field knowing they gave everything they had, played as well as they could, and exemplified sportsmanship, I promise you they will walk off with peace of mind and their heads held high. That in my estimation is a winner.

photo: Sacramento Bee

Some of the boys' team rooting during the girls' play-offs.

CHAPTER 2

WINNING AND LOSING

Our goal is not to win. It's to play together and play hard. Then, winning takes care of itself.
— Mike Krzyzewski

It is important to note here that the final score should have very little role in determining the success of a game. For example, my 1994 baseball team was really giving it to one of our league opponents, Victory Christian. We ended up winning 16-0. Before and during the game, though, I really felt we weren't prepared to play. We didn't give it our best effort, and we weren't focused on the game. I personally believe that is showing disrespect for your opponent and the sport. I tried to bring the intensity level up throughout, but because of the one-sidedness of the contest, I didn't have much success. Well, to say the least, a number of players were very surprised with the twenty minute tongue lashing they received after the game. Some of them couldn't understand how I could be so upset because we had won 16-0. Remember, it's not about the final score. A number of players who were on that team who graduated in the class of '95 have shared with me that that game and subsequent team meetings afterwards really helped mold their own philosophies of what is truly important about sports.

Here's another example. My '91 basketball team was my best ever. That particular season we beat three top ten teams in the area (the area being all of Sacramento at any division) and were rated third in the state for all Division 5 schools. However, one of my proudest moments with this team didn't come with an upset win of a top ranked team, but with a hard fought loss to Milpitas, an outstanding Bay Area school. They were clearly the superior team, much bigger and much deeper, but we never gave in. We battled to the final buzzer. It was truly an inspiration to me and to everyone watching the game. Total strangers came up to me to congratulate me on having such a fine team. We played to our highest level, gave everything we had, and played with true sportsmanship.

As a coach, I had to acknowledge this to my players. I couldn't have been more proud if they had won the game. I couldn't belittle this accomplishment by saying things such as, if only we made more shots or had fewer turnovers, or done this or done that. Celebrate such occasions and take advantage of the opportunity to teach and ingrain in your players the true meaning of sport and competition. My players were winners on that night, which paved the way for a championship season in more ways than one.

There are great lessons to be learned from both winning and losing. Seeing all of your hard work and commitment pay off with success is a great motivator for all aspects of life. Continually I see student athletes apply discipline that they learned and/or refined in team sports to other endeavors in life, such as school work, jobs, or even fitness goals. Failure is also an important teacher. You can grow stronger physically and mentally through adversity. To know that you can give your best effort and still not win can be a valuable lesson. It prepares you for the struggle that life has in store. It also teaches you that the most important thing is not the scoreboard. Again, it goes back to giving everything you are capable of, and if that isn't good enough, it's okay. You are still as successful as anyone else. No one can ask for more than that.

So how do you bring about strong attitude and effort? How do you ensure that the students are competing for the right reasons? It helps significantly to instill the right ethics and morals in your children regarding sports as you raise them, but the coach can't be underestimated. In my twenty years of organized sports as a player, and twelve years in the coaching profession, I have had countless coaches to draw from and shape my foundation of coaching philosophy. Unfortunately, for me, most of what I received was ways of how not to do it. This, still, was very important in my forming of ideas. I grew up in an era of negative motivation. Coaches felt that the best way to motivate someone was to berate him. I have to admit that this worked on me very well when I played. I wanted to show these coaches that I could do it, so I pushed even harder. However, I have often wondered what it would have been like to play for someone who was always positive and who took a great interest in his players' lives. I grew up hearing, "You can't get too close to your players." Yes, there need to be some boundaries, but I feel you can have very close relationships with your players and still have their respect and attention.

Waves' Julie Umphenour shows off her perfect form.

CHAPTER 3

COMPETITION AT WHAT AGE?
HOW EARLY IS TOO EARLY?

Until now, I have written about competition and how it should be brought in the high school. But what about the younger kids? According to the National Youth Sports Coaches, almost 20 million children play a team sport before high school. Of that number, 75 percent who start at age 6 or 7 will quit before they are 15. So, how young is too young?

Kischnick states, "There are worlds of difference that lie between the single years of life." I think we have to be very conscious of this fact when we look into sports. He goes on further to say,

> In the second seven year period of the child, he starts off with beauty or harmony. The responsibility of the teacher or coach for the young people in his care, when keeping this perspective in mind, is obviously very great, He needs to teach in a way that brings reverence to the child's virtues.

Kischnick also states: "All physical education has to be at the same time moral education." The same, I believe, can be said for sports. "If one allows children to play sports while moral forces do not carry the movement," Kischnick adds, "one surrenders them to the forces of the earth. The body hardens, the heart wastes away and the spirit dries up. "

At the Sacramento Waldorf School, the earliest our students participate in organized athletic competition is junior high, and this is only on a very limited basis. The seventh and eighth graders join other area Waldorf schools for a yearly track meet and recently have joined a basketball league.

I have often thought of the possible connection between Kischnick's statements and my basketball program. We had never had any junior high basketball until the last four years. This meant that virtually all of the players I coached when they entered ninth grade had never played organized basketball. The only experiences they had were out on the blacktop at lunch and recess. And yet, to this day, the best players that I've ever had, the best teams that I've ever coached, have all come from this period. How can this be explained? I think the main reasons the players who hadn't had any organized athletic experience excelled so greatly are: they didn't play at an early age which could have led them to be a part of that 75 percent burnout statistic; they were very eager and open to learning; and they were taught and coached in a way that did add reverence to their virtues.

It's important to note that over the last four years—the time since we started a junior high program—we have still been successful. We have still won league championships and reached the section and Nor-Cal playoffs, but I haven't seen as much individual improvement, or possibly as great a love of the sport, in a child who started in junior high or earlier as I have in those who did not start until high school.

In conclusion, I believe the student athlete can benefit in many ways by waiting until he or she is in high school before competing in team sports. However, children can still have a very healthy and positive experience starting at a younger age as long as they are in a program that will develop their skills and love for the movement without the hardening of the body, mind, and spirit.

CHAPTER 4

THE ROLE OF THE COACH

What lies before us and what lies behind us are small matters compared to what lies within us. And when we bring what is within out into the world, miracles happen.

— Henry David Thoreau

The role that a coach plays for a team should be very broad. Some of the most important characteristics a good coach can provide to a team are: being a positive role model; giving unity to his team; providing powerful motivation, preparation, and organization; being respectful of others and deserving respect in return; and being knowledgeable in the specific field.

Being a Role Model

One hundred years from now it will not matter what kind of car I drove, what kind of house I lived in, how much money I had in my bank account, nor what my clothes looked like. But the world may be a little better because I was important in the life of a child.

— Author Unknown

Nothing has made me more proud than to have some of my former players turn to the coaching profession as a livelihood. To know that I have been a positive influence in their lives is a very special feeling.

Being in this position to influence young people shouldn't be taken lightly. In fact, it is a big responsibility. Eyes are on you all of the time. Because of this, coaches should make their best effort to be fit, eat healthily, and live the virtues of their sport, not just speak them. You don't have to be fit or be a vegetarian to be an excellent coach, but I think it's easier for your players to be proud of you if you take pride in yourself.

Coaches have a great opportunity to preach the virtues of a healthy diet. Too many times, I've seen coaches guzzling down coffee and doughnuts, smoking cigarettes, and "slamming" cheeseburgers and fries. You have to remember that you're in a position to guide their choices. Take advantage of that. I know my players appreciate the fact that I work out regularly, eat healthily, and dress nicely for games.

Your players also need to know that you are a fair, honest, upright person, who is consistently striving for excellence. It's very important to be what you say. If you are always on your players to be level-headed in games, and you're ranting and raving on the sidelines, you lose your credibility. Whatever your aspirations are for your players, you should live yourself. Remember: practice what you preach.

Team Unity

The main ingredient in stardom is the rest of the team.
— Author Unknown

Without a doubt, your team will never reach its potential if it isn't united. Every member has to have the attitude that the team comes first.

In the 1989-90 season, I had a very young team. I started two juniors and three sophomores. Nothing was expected of this team outside of playing hard every day. However, my best player, Colin Poer, had a dream season; he averaged 26 points a game and led us to 20 wins and to the league title. The following season was going to be one of huge expectation. I knew, though, if we were a one man team, we wouldn't live up to all of the hoopla surrounding us. I spoke with Colin in the off season about individual and team goals and how we could accomplish our objectives for the upcoming season. We both felt that if the scoring was spread around, we would be much tougher to stop. Even though he had dreams of leading the area in scoring and earning numerous individual awards, he put his teammates above himself. He still averaged 20 points a game but we had three other players in double figures, and led by Colin and Andy Goncalves, we had our most successful season in school history.

Team unity is not just about your starters' being unselfish. Equally important is the role your bench players play. During this history making season, I also had a group of non-starters who had a big impact on our success. Jon (J-Dub) White was a team reserve who seldom got to play in a close game. But he, probably more than any other player in the history of our school, exemplified the true meaning of a team player. His constant, unconditional support for his team throughout the year and throughout his career were inspiring to everyone. He made a lasting impression on his teammates and coach and helped insure the success of the club. He did this by always cheering for his teammates, always giving his all in practice and in the games he played, and by always exuding pride in being a member of the team.

It's very important as a coach to discuss with your bench players their individual role. If this is explained early on, it will prevent a lot of problems. J-Dub knew exactly where he stood. Although some roles may be the same, all players have roles. I personally feel comfortable only playing 6-8 players in a game, until the contest has been decided. Your players also need to know that they have the opportunity to change their role with their attitude, hustle, and play. On numerous occasions, I have had bench players move up to being starters, and starters move down to the bench, through the individual's attitude and performance.

Whatever the means, you as a coach can play an integral role in uniting your team and making an unforgettable season. What turned out to be very powerful for me one year was a "team night." My team (1993-94 basketball) chose to get together one night every week and just hang out. We went to movies, played pool, watched game films, whatever. It really brought the feeling of togetherness and helped significantly in our championship season.

As I will discuss later, a team covenant can be very helpful.

Motivation

You know, we can't get out of life alive! We can either die in the bleachers or die on the field. We might as well come down on the field and go for it!
— Les Brown

Another important characteristic of a good coach is being able to motivate. Every successful coach I know is a powerful motivator. It's what raises teams and coaches from average to elite. There are a lot of coaches out there who know the "Xs and Os" like the back of their hand but they can't quite get their players to play to their full potential.

Coaches have to make the sport special. Motivation is the key to unlocking that potential. Players need to be continuously reminded of why they're working so hard. The coach needs to create an atmosphere where the players are continuously striving to achieve. Remind the players regularly about the team goals that have been set. Encourage your players consistently about giving their all.

Over the last twelve years, I have learned what it takes to really motivate a team. I am continuously thinking about new ways to inspire, but here are a few ways that I guarantee will work.

Goal Setting

> *You cannot stay on the summit forever;*
> *You have to come down again.*
> *so why bother in the first place?*
> *Because what is below does not know what is above,*
> *but what is above knows what is below.*
> *One climbs, one sees.*
> *One descends, one sees no longer,*
> *But one has seen.*
> *There is an art of conducting oneself*
> *In the lower regions*
> *By the memory of what one saw higher up.*
> *When one can no longer see,*
> *One can at least still know.*

— Mt. Analogue

Every team needs to have clear, defined goals for what they want to accomplish. I believe the best setting for this is a team gathering at one of the players' homes, preferably the first or second week of the season. That timing is important because, if the team has had a few days together, they will already be forming a bond and they will have some experience to draw on when thinking of ways to make things better.

In setting goals, the coach plays a big part in guiding the team's discussion. He needs to insure that his players are striving for the right things. One of the worst things you could do as a coach is set only lofty or potentially unattainable goals. What happens to a team whose only goals are to go undefeated and win the league championship if they lose a couple of games during the beginning of the season? The possibility of their giving up or looking at their season as a disappointment is increased. Our team goals may have those mentioned above, but they're way down on the list. Make sure that your list includes goals such as: having fun, being positive, being united as a team, and so forth.

Team Covenant

What we have done in the past is draw up a team covenant. (See example opposite.) I got this idea from one of the top coaches around today, Pat Riley. A covenant is basically an agreement that binds people together. It comes from the entire team's input and everyone has to agree with it. When it's finished, everyone signs it and everyone gets a copy. We came out of our first team meeting in '94 so fired up and so in tune as to our mission for the season that nothing could have stopped us that year. I'm telling you now that this is powerful stuff.

Dean Strunk

WAVES BASKETBALL
Team Covenant — our agreement to bind us together

I. COMMITMENT
 A. mentally prepared & focussed for each practice & game
 B. give it everything we have for each practice & game
 C. decide on daily intention in the morning & be conscious
 of it throughout the entire school day & practice

II. TEAM UNITY
 A. everyone is positive—no negative comments from team-
 mates
 B. everyone makes practice
 C. we can count on each other for anything
 D. team concept night—we meet as a group every Monday
 night

III. OBSTACLES
 A. Physical: injuries, sickness
 B. School: academic, behavioral problems
 C. Social: girl friend/boy friend, family troubles

IV. SOLUTIONS — "finding a way"
 A. Physical: get a lot of sleep, eat right, think positively
 B. School: set time for homework, ask for help from teach-
 ers/peers
 C. Social: Have/find someone you can talk to about any-
 thing
 E Resources for solutions: teammates, friends, family,
 coach

17

Daily Intentions

In each of us are heroes. Speak to them and they will come forth.
— Anonymous

Another positive way to motivate through goal setting is to have your players write out their daily intentions. For years, my players have written down their individual and team goals, signed them, and given them to me. This is a great ritual, and my players continue to do this—but I have realized that these goals don't live in some of the players on a daily basis. With the daily intentions exercise, however, I have found that my players are much more conscious of their goals on a regular basis. At every practice, my players give me a signed list of intentions that they want to accomplish. The list can be as short or as long as they want. A few examples could be: I am going to go as hard as I can on every

It's a beautiful day for baseball as Waves' Austin Maydahl warms up his pitcher.

Waves players battle for the ball.

drill. I will show no negative emotion. I will be mentally pre-pared for today's practice, and so on. This is a great way to have your players prepare themselves ahead of time for the upcoming practice or game. I remember Andy, who during my pre-game talks of our playoff run in '91, would throw down a pad of paper at my feet with his intentions on it. He was letting me know (not so subtly) that my point guard was ready to play. I promise you, if you try this, your consistency of intensity will never be better.

WEEKLY JOURNAL

One of the most recent ideas I've had with regard to motivating players is a weekly journal. (See over.) A weekly journal is a form that your players use to chart their own performances. Whereas my other ideas are geared to pump up or prepare my players for the upcoming practice or game, the weekly journal is unique in that it enables my players to reflect upon their performance after the practice or game is over and critique what they did well and what they can improve upon. My players found this tool very helpful in bringing greater insight into their connection with preparation and performance.

WEEKLY IMPROVEMENT JOURNAL

WEEK OF:_____

QUESTIONS TO ASK YOURSELF:
                Did I arrive mentally prepared?
                Did I go as hard as I could?
                Did I have a positive attitude?
                What can I do better?

Monday	Tuesday	Wednesday	Thursday	Friday	Saturday

Daily Quote and Word of Emphasis

A couple years ago, I decided to add something to my practices. Always striving to motivate my players, I included a word of emphasis and a daily quote. I chose a word that I wanted to be the focal point of the practice (example: enthusiasm). Then I found a quote that I felt properly defined the enthusiasm that I was looking for (example: Nothing great was ever achieved without enthusiasm. — Ralph Waldo Emerson). Don't underestimate this tool. The day I realized I had something was with the first team I tried it with—1993-94 basketball. I had been doing it for a few weeks, and I thought it was going pretty well. On one particular day I was in the middle of saying "And today's quote is by . . . " when suddenly the J.V. team, practicing on the other end of the court, started their lay-up drills with balls bouncing all over the place, making a lot of noise. In unison, my entire team turned around and yelled, "Hold the balls!" They wanted their quote to help motivate them for the start of practice.

Final Thoughts on Motivation

I have mentioned a number of ways to help motivate your team. None of these techniques will work for you fully, though, if you don't instill them with enthusiasm. Your players need to see and believe that you love what you do. You have to be passionate about your job. I hate to even call it a job. I think life's work sounds a lot better. If you put a lot of energy and enthusiasm into your life's work, you can't help but motivate the people around you and be happier to boot. Remember: Nothing great was ever achieved without enthusiasm.

Being Prepared and Organized

It's better to prepare for an opportunity that may never come than to have an opportunity but find ourselves unprepared.
— Les Brown

I will get ready and perhaps my chance will come.
— Author Unknown

This part of coaching can't be overlooked. It's one of the things I've had to work hardest on. If you're not organized, your players will know. My players have a sense of security in knowing that their entire practice is scheduled out, on paper, down to the minute. (See sample opposite.) It tells them that I have been thinking about what we are going to do today, and they know that things will run smoothly. If you are just winging it or saying "Let's scrimmage" all of the time, your players will sense that you aren't putting in a lot of preparation for your practices. Remember, if you're going to ask your players to show up mentally prepared, you had better make sure that you do the same.

Getting ready to bring the heat.

BASKETBALL PRACTICE

Word of Emphasis — team
Quote: It's amazing how much can be accomplished if no one cares who receives the credit.

Minutes

5	talk
6	layups
1	Defensive stance
1	Directional footwork
2	Positive pivots/close outs
1	1 & 1 free throws
8	Shell drill
6	Switch drill
1	1 & 1 free throws

run & jump full court pressing, defensive breakdown drills.

1	1 on 1
1	2 on 1
4	2 on 2
4	3 on 3
4	4 on 3
8	5 on 5

1	1 & 1 free throws
7	Post moves, triple threats (perimeter work)
8	Man offense 5-0
10	man off. 5-5 (scrimmage)
1	1 & 1 free throws
1	skip passes
8	Zone off. (5-0)
8	Zone off (5-5 scrimmage)
8	Conditioning
8	Free throws

Respect

If each of us sweeps in front of our own steps, the whole world will be clean.

— Goethe

It's very important for the players to respect the coach. They can disagree with him and maybe not even care for him deeply, but they still need to have respect for him. This goes double for the coach respecting the player.

Some people feel you have to earn respect, and that's okay. I personally respect everyone, unless he gives me a reason not to. I also believe I will earn anyone's respect by being an honest, sincere, upright person, and by being committed to doing a good job teaching and coaching. Strive to be a role model, and the respect will be there.

Knowledge

It is what you learn after you know it all that counts.

— John Wooden

Strive to be an expert in your field. There are many avenues to pursue to learn your craft. Clinics, books, tapes, and other coaches are all great resources to take advantage of. When I started coaching basketball in 1985, 1 didn't have a clue. Because of a knee injury, I had played only one year of high school basketball and never really followed the game that closely either. I told the administration at the Sacramento Waldorf School that I was interested in the position and, because there was no one on campus more qualified, I got the job. It only took two or three games for me to realize that I was in way over my head. Most coaches start out as an assistant, or coach a junior high team, or a freshman team, and learn from the head varsity coach. Well, I didn't have that luxury. I was the head varsity coach. So, very early on, I decided I could get pummeled year after year, or I could study and improve. I opted for the latter. I sought out as many coaches as I could. I read book after book, I went to clinic after clinic, and I got better. It took four years of continuously striving to improve my craft before I felt a little comfortable about what I was doing. That year coincided with our first ever league championship. We have added five more in the last seven years. I have a great deal of pride in what I've accomplished, especially knowing where I started. I am continuing to learn every year, and I know I still have a great deal to learn. Knowledge is a never ending Journey. Seek the path with passion.

Developing Your Own Philosophy

My goal as a coach is to make each season the most special experience ever in the lives of my players.
— Dean Stark

Life's experiences play a big part in shaping your personality. The same can be said about shaping your coaching philosophy. I've written about the role of a coach and the qualities he should possess and impart to his team. Those same qualities and ideals are, in fact, a big part of coaching. Every coach should have a foundation of beliefs and principles that make up his own philosophy You as a coach should seek out successful people in your field to help you form your foundation. You should continually be eager to learn.

Go to clinics, read books, watch tapes. Be thirsty for knowledge, but make sure you mold a philosophy that is true for you. Be yourself. Just because some successful coaches berate their players doesn't mean you have to. And remember: it's easy to spot a fake. If what you say or do is not coming from your heart, your players will know.

Sport Specialization

It seems as though every basketball program around these days is a year-round program. Right after the "season", the players are off to spring league, then summer league, team camps, summer weight training and conditioning programs, fall league, and then back to practice for the next season. There is never a break. In fact, there is no "off" season any more. More and more coaches are emphasizing specialization in a particular sport, either by discouraging their players from playing anything else, or by offering an alternative such as a spring league which conflicts with the spring sport offered by the school. And it's not just basketball. Football, baseball, and volleyball are other sports developing year-round programs as well.

When I played in high school, students were always encouraged to play anything they wanted to. We had a solid number of athletes who participated in two or more sports. Usually the athlete himself would choose which sport(s) to stick with based on enjoyment, success, and coaching. Now I feel that coaches are forcing the players' hands. They are making them stick to one sport or risk losing a starting position or playing time in that sport. This isn't healthy.

I think coaches, in general, have lost sight of the true essence of sport. Sports weren't created for coaches. It's not about how many league titles the coach can win, how many "coach of the year" awards are attained, or what the career winning percentage is. I have to admit that I have struggled with this. I came into coaching very goal-oriented and these things were high on my list of priorities. After a number of years, I really thought I had distanced myself from the focus on winning and trophies, but the prospect of losing really challenged my views and beliefs. I learned that I didn't really test my philosophy of coaching when I was winning. It's very easy to say winning isn't the most important thing when you are always victorious. The real test was: not winning and still holding firm to my beliefs. Furthermore, because of year-round programs and sport specialization in other schools, the stark reality (a little play on words there) was that I would either have to sacrifice my beliefs and join all of the other schools in year-round play to insure the continued success of my program, or stay true to my values, risk losing, but know what I was doing was in the best interest of the personal development of the player.

I decided that the best solution for me, my players, and the other team sports on our campus was not to offer any type of program while another school sport was going on. This insured that there would be no pressure on any athlete to choose between the two. I also opened up the opportunity for my players to participate in a summer league if they wanted to, knowing there would be no pressure on them to attend. This helped by allowing us to feel we weren't too far behind everyone else in what they were doing. We got to play a couple times a week for six weeks against good competition to help prepare us for next year. It worked out wonderfully. The players who wanted to play did, and the players who couldn't make it, for whatever reason, knew that was okay, too.

Coaches have to hold to their beliefs and virtues. Basing all decisions on winning sets you up for disappointment and, in the long run, a lack of credibility.

Playing Time

Quite possibly, the biggest problem a coach will face year in and year out is finding playing time for his bench players. I know a number of coaches who have left the profession entirely because they were so fed up with parents' complaining about their son's or daughter's not having a chance to play. As a coach, if you are worried about getting a player into a game because you don't want to deal with his or her father (or mother) afterwards, you probably haven't done a good job in communicating with players and parents. In all of my years of coaching, I have only had two parents come up to me and ask for an explanation of why their son was not playing more.

There are several things you can do to help alleviate this situation. As I mentioned earlier in this chapter, meeting with each player and discussing his role is vital. If your players are clear as to their place on the team, they will be united with you. Again, they don't have to like it and they need to know they can change it through attitude, effort, and performance, but it is very important that they understand and accept their role. If your players do, their parents usually will as well.

Having a meeting with the parents of your players at the beginning of your season is also a good way to deal with the playing time issue. Sit down with them and discuss your philosophy. This will help immensely.

Another thing you can do to ease the playing time dilemma is pre-setting your substitution patterns before the game. For example, in basketball, a coach could notify his subs that they will enter the game at specific times during the contest, regardless of the situation. By taking this approach you ensure that your players will get a set amount of game time. I have known coaches who have had entire units of five players sub in at set times in each game throughout the entire season.

My philosophy on this subject is: no player is guaranteed playing time. A player earns his minutes by showing up to practice consistently, playing hard, and having a positive attitude. Someone who does these things at the junior high level should play in every game, regardless of skill level. The same generally holds true at the junior varsity level (ninth and tenth grades). The exception would be a case when you might put a player into a situation where he will almost certainly fail. Sometimes it is worse to play someone when he is not physically and mentally ready. This is especially true at the varsity level. Sometimes we have games in front of seven or eight hundred people, games that come down to the final possession, games in which my players are under a lot of pressure. Putting a player in a situation like that when he is not ready is a big risk. The odds of his failing are high and so are the chances of his feeling that he let his teammates down. At the varsity level, showing up to practice on time, hustling, and having a positive attitude only give a player the opportunity to play. Skill level must be considered also. I would love to get all of my players into the game. Virtually every year all of my players do accomplish the "opportunity" requirements, but that doesn't mean they are guaranteed to have playing time. If your players and their parents know this early you are going to save yourself a lot of headaches.

Waves on three: one, two, three, Waves!

CHAPTER 5

ON THE SIDELINES

Practice, Pre-game, and Games

At practice, there are no time outs, no subs. And no excuses. You just go flat out until it's over and if you want to wear the uniform bad enough it's never over...

— Michael Jordan

I mentioned in Chapter 4 about the importance of being prepared and organized. I would like to expand on this by breaking down the actual practice session into two parts: planning and practice. I will use basketball as an example.

Planning—An Overview

I have a general idea of how I want our season to unfold. I have certain things that we need to cover by the time we play our first game and certain things that need to be covered by the time we start our league season. For example: during the early part of the season, we work mainly on our basic offenses, man to man defense, out-of-bounds plays, and conditioning. These aspects of our game need to be solid before our first contest. As we move closer to our conference opener, we add quick hitters, trapping defenses, and other special situation plays. One advantage to doing these as you go is that other coaches who scout you in the preseason will not have seen your entire system. By approaching your season this way, you will find that your players are not overloaded with too many things to learn all at once and it gives you more time to concentrate on fundamentals early in the year, which is critical for your team's success.

31

Another idea that may help your planning is keeping a journal of every practice. Basically, this means writing down everything you do each day, including effort and enthusiasm which was given and received, the quality of the practice, and other details you notice.

I just started keeping track of all our practices. I'm looking forward to referring to my notes next season to see where we'll be compared to this year. I hope I will be able to add to next season's practices by borrowing from this year. It will be nice to have the notes, to look back at what worked well and what could be improved upon. Furthermore, I can see how this will help years down the road after I've compiled files of a number of teams. Each team has its own style, which dictates how I coach, and having files on different styles will give me quick access to what worked with a similar team in the past.

Practice

Practice is the most important key to the success of your team. Very seldom, if ever, are you going to find a team so talented that it doesn't need to practice soundly to win. John Wooden, the all-time great coach from UCLA who won more national championships (ten) than anyone else in the college game, said in his book *They Call Me Coach* that, "More than likely any league championship or post-season success will be a result of the quality work done on the practice floor." At Sacramento Waldorf, we only practice four days a week so I need to make sure that the time my players spend is used very well.

First of all, I fully prepare for each practice. I need to be able to demonstrate each drill, play, and fundamental with skill, enthusiasm, and confidence. Secondly, I teach drills of a short duration.

Our drills last anywhere from 1-10 minutes. It's important to keep things moving briskly. It's also important to have the right person demonstrating the drills. Make sure the person (player or coach) knows how to do them properly. You don't want someone teaching the wrong form. Also, don't spend too much time explaining a drill or play. What works for me is to demonstrate, have a short explanation, and then practice it.

Another helpful hint is to alternate difficult (physically taxing) drills with less difficult drills. For example, I want to do shooting drills right after a full court defensive or conditioning drill. This creates a game-like situation for shooting because my players are fatigued and breathing hard. Shooting one-and-one free throws is also a good drill to do after your team is winded.

One final question for structuring practice is: how to end it. Coach Wooden said that he always tried to finish practice on a positive note. I totally agree. It's probably the last thing your players are going to remember and you want them to go home happy and excited about coming back the next day. Take advantage of this time by complimenting their effort and pointing out their improvement.

Pre-game Rituals

I have thought a lot about pre-game rituals and what works best for a team. I am going to use basketball as an example. And when I say pre-game, that doesn't mean just arriving an hour and a half before tip-off to get ready. Pre-game for me starts at practice the day before. I believe a team plays the way it practices, so my team needs to know that our practice time is vital to our success. It is at practice that we will go over our scouting report on our opposition. More on that later. It's also a time when I ask them to think about tomorrow's game tonight, before they go to bed. I want them to picture all of the things that we practiced and prepared for. I want them to think of the next morning as Christmas day—that they can't wait to get up because it's game day and they get an opportunity to play the game that they love. It makes me feel great (and confident) when my players walk by and say "Christmas Day, baby!" or "Merry Christmas, Coach!"

Mental preparation is also a very important element of our pregame ritual. This, too, starts the day before. I make sure to remind my players at the end of our practice of all of the things they need to be thinking about. Here's my list and brief description of each: 1. Game time and when we need to be at the gym; 2. What uniform we're wearing (home or away); 3. Transportation information; 4. What to do from 3:15 p.m. (school dismissal) to 6:00 p.m.; and, 5. When and what to eat.

School Dismissal

My players have just under three hours from the time school gets out to the time they need to be at the gym. I want them to relax, quiet their mind, and visualize everything that could happen in the game. I also want them to take a shower. This may sound weird, but there's something about taking a shower before a game that not only wakes you up, but pumps you up as well. As for when to arrive at the gym, I have had a long-standing rule that we need to be there an hour and a half before tip-off. However, I may look at altering this slightly. Our girls team plays right before us and a number of my players have said that they get lethargic watching a game before they play. Now this has nothing to do with our girls team because they are an outstanding team, and they play hard and are exciting to watch. However, as they have become stronger, many of their league games have become somewhat one-sided. Watching such games can make it hard sometimes to keep focused. Yet it's also important to show our support to our girls team, so I'm still working on this one. I may try a 6:15 arrival time next year and see how that goes.

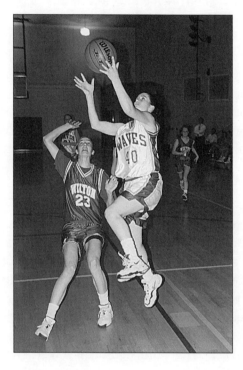

Waves' Emmi Connolly drives to the hoop.

When and What To Eat

First of all, before I give you a list of things to eat before and after a contest, I want to take the time to emphasize how vital good nutrition is, not only to your future performance, but also to your future health and well-being. If I could give you any advice about nutrition, it would be to eat foods that are low in fat, salt, and sugar, to avoid or limit intake of meat (especially red meat), to eat foods that are high in fiber, to eat organic fruits and vegetables whenever possible, and to take daily supplements, including a complete multi-vitamin/multi-mineral/multi-antioxidant. It is also important to drink clean water. Dr. Michael Colgan, in his best selling book *The New Nutrition* states that:

> Your muscles are seventy percent water. Your blood is 82% water. Even your bones are a quarter water. This basic biochemistry emphasizes that the most important component of your body is plain H2O. The quality of your muscles, bones, organs, and brain, their biochemistry, their resistance to injury and disease, and their longevity, is absolutely dependent on the purity of the water you drink.

So drink water and make sure it's clean. The purest form is distilled. And for athletes, this is especially important. Vigorous exercise dehydrates the body. Colgan writes that "When a muscle is dehydrated by only 3% you cause about 10% loss of contractile strength, and an 8% loss of speed. Performance literally dries up." So if you want optimum performance for your players, make sure you keep them hydrated.

Back to pre-game meals. This information is taken from Dr. Robert Haas, one of the leading sports nutritionists in the world today. In his book *Eat To Win*, Haas says,

> Don't eat a large meal before competition or exercise. Your body cannot perform at it's best if your stomach is overloaded with fats, protein, and carbohydrates. Since physical activity severely retards digestion, you should go into battle with a lean and hungry look. Keep food intake to a minimum to satisfy hunger (no more that 250 kilocalories, if possible). This is equivalent to about 4

slices of whole grain bread or 1/4 cup of whole grain cereal with 1/2 cup of skimmed milk and 1 fresh fruit. Wait at least two hours after eating before beginning your favorite sport or exercise.

Your precompetition meal should consist primarily of complex carbohydrates (about 60-80% of the kilocalories in your pregame meal should come from whole grains, cereals, fruits, breads, pasta, and vegetables).

And, obviously, drink lots of water. Haas says that an athlete should "drink at least 1 cup of water for every 50 pounds of body weight before he begins physical activity. Then drink at least 1 cup of water (8 ounces) for every 15 minutes of physical activity."

Your Post-competition Meal

Again, this information was taken from Haas' book *Eat To Win*.

This meal must do two things for you: 1. Give you the nutritional building blocks to restore the glycogen your muscles have burned during exercise, and; 2. Replace the fluid, vitamins, minerals, and protein your body needs every day.

A recommended post-game meal might be:
1. Four ounces of fish or poultry.
2. Two baked or boiled potatoes or 1 cup of cooked pasta with plain tomato or marinara sauce.
3. One cup of green, yellow, or orange steamed or raw vegetables uch as broccoli, hard yellow squash, or carrots.
4. Two fresh tropical or citrus fruits.
5. Water according to thirst, plus at least 1 additional pint.

Transportation

We travel to our away games by car. We go over our travel itinerary to simply make sure everyone knows how we're getting there, who is driving, when we're leaving and when we'll probably be home. Going over it a day before makes it just one less thing for your players to worry about and gives their parents a clear picture of the evening. It's also important to remind your players if you are going to stop for food on the way home from the game so they can plan to bring money with them.

Things We Need To Do To Be Successful

I talk day in and day out about the same things that make a successful team. Offensive and defensive fundamentals, team play, and playing with heart and passion. These are constants. In preparing for a particular opponent, though, I need to be more specific. For example, if we're playing a team that presses and traps all over the court, we need to be prepared to deal with that and know how to attack it. Your team needs to be ready for anything that your opponent may throw at you. This leads me to the next topic—knowing your opponent.

Scouting

Scouting is a tool to use in preparing your team for a particular opponent. I probably scout less than most coaches, but that doesn't mean that I don't think it's important. My goal in scouting is to have a general idea of what the other team is going to do and know the individual strengths and weaknesses of their players. For example, I want to know what defenses the other team uses. Do they press? Are they a fast- breaking team? Are they a perimeter shooting team? Do they pound it inside? Which individuals on their team shoot the best, attack the basket off the dribble?

Can they drive with their weak hand? I feel if I have this information that's all I really need to know. I think it's more important to spend your valuable practice time on developing your own team. Again, I fall in line with Coach Wooden who said when commenting on scouting, "I will prepare my players the best I can and I'll let the other team worry about us."

Basketball Lunch

A new idea I am looking forward to trying is: on game day my team will meet and have lunch together. We may talk a little about our game. We may have a different teammate each time make a presentation about what basketball means to him or something along those lines, or we may just eat together. It's another way to grow closer as a team and mentally prepare for our game.

In the Locker Room

Okay. You had a solid practice yesterday. At night, you thought about what you needed to do to be successful in your game. You wake up thinking it is Christmas day. You went home after school and relaxed, visualized, and even showered. You had your pre-game meal. You show up with the right uniform at the right time.

Now what? What's left is the actual pre-game period. My players go into the locker room (actually it's a classroom at our school) after our girls come out of the same room during halftime and just before the start of the third quarter of their game. My players put on their uniforms, stretch, and wait for me to come in.

Speaking of uniforms, there was a trend starting at our school that I squelched and I suggest you do the same if it happens at yours. Our players for different sports started showing up to school wearing their uniforms (usually under their school clothes). They were showing their school spirit. What I believe they were doing was taking away the thrill and excitement of putting on their uniform right before a game. That was always one of my highlights as a player. It also should be part of one's mental preparation. I will never forget a former player of mine, John Beaven, while putting on his basketball jersey would claim, "I am now The Beavenator." And then he would go back it up on the court. Don't let anything diminish the pre-game dressing ritual.

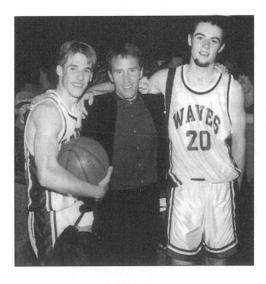

Coach Stark celebrates with Brian Barboza (left) and John Beaven after knocking off defending section champion Ripon Christian.

Back to the pre-game. I come in and wait to make sure everyone is finished dressing. As a coach, this is a very important time. I need to be very confident and articulate. I also want to speak a little more quickly than usual. I think my players retain more of what I say that way. I don't want to appear nervous or overly excited. I believe my players will follow my lead. I will restate our game plan and remind my players of our keys to the game.

Sometimes I will do something a little different but generally I like to keep the same rhythm to our pre-game. What I don't want to do is to stir my team's emotions into a frenzy. It's a mistake getting your players too hyped before the game. I want my players to treat every game the same. We're playing a nameless, faceless opponent, and our goal is to play at our highest level.

Game Time

If you and your players have prepared properly both on and off the court, the game will be the positive result of that preparation. It's a wonderful thing to see your players execute the game plan out on the floor. It demonstrates that what you are doing is working. The game will also tell you what part of your team development still needs addressing.

Time-outs

What can you do if your game plan isn't working? My best advice is to figure out why. A coach should be ready to make any needed adjustments during the course of a game. One way to do this is through time-outs. I personally don't like to use time-outs unless I have to. I want to save them for the end when I may really need them. I feel that my team is going to be the better conditioned team and taking a time-out will give our opponents an opportunity to rest and catch their breath. Sometimes, though, a coach has no other choice. I will use my time-outs to stop a run from the other team, to diagram a play, to change defenses, or maybe just to try to get a little more effort out of my squad. During time-outs, a coach needs to be in control. He has to be very clear in his instructions to his team. Everyone needs to be on the same page; and if a coach has assistants, it's important that all the staff members know their roles. There's nothing more confusing than three coaches talking at the same time. For me, what works is: after I finish talking, my assistants add their input.

Coach Stark centers his team during a time-out.

Halftime

Halftime can be a big advantage if you use it wisely. How many times have you seen a team being soundly beaten after two periods and then making an incredible comeback after halftime? It happens. Just this past season, I watched our girls team come back from a seventeen point halftime deficit and win against a talented team. Announcers on television, after a team makes a great second half run to get back into the game, always comment that the coach must have really let his team have it at halftime. This is sometimes true, but definitely not always the case. I must admit there have been times when I lit into my team, but it has always depended on the circumstances and not the score. The one thing that I can't tolerate is lack of effort, and if my players are giving what I perceive to be less than 100% effort, you can bet they are going to hear about it. I believe this is all right from time to time if you have your team's trust and respect. In fact, my former players often recall those seven minute tongue lashings very fondly when we get together. (I guess time does heal a lot.)

Usually, though, my halftime talks are conversations with my players. My assistants and I will point out things that we can do a little better or things we can take advantage of, and my players will offer their insights into the contest, as they often give helpful input to our game plan. Using this time in this way will ensure that everyone on your team is unified and prepared for the second half of the game.

Post-game

As I mentioned earlier in this chapter, in structuring practice it's important to finish the day with something positive. This is one of my main goals for my post-game talk. If my team is down, I want to raise their spirits. I may speak a little about some of the things we could have done better, but mostly I will acknowledge the good things that came from the game and make sure they leave the room with their heads held high.

There is a rare occasion, however, when I may be hard on my team. Again, it comes down to effort and attitude. If my players aren't giving it their all, they will be held accountable. They need to know this. There is no gray area. They will respect you more knowing that you hold them to their highest selves.

Now, if your team has done very well, it's important to acknowledge their efforts, but also to keep it in perspective. I still want them to have their feet on the ground. There is always room for improvement.

All in all, after a game, I don't want my team too dejected over a loss or too elated over a win. I want them to be able to say they played to their best ability, gave it everything they had, and I want them to walk out standing tall.

A coach needs to be focused, knowledgeable, and prepared.

CHAPTER 6

A COACH'S LIST

Coaching is still more art than science.

— Chuck Daly

Ever since I wrote the first edition of this book, *Coaching Team Sports in a Waldorf School*, I have heard from a number of Waldorf coaches all over the country. They have asked me questions concerning a lot of different areas, some of which I will address here.

Making Mistakes

Every coach is going to make mistakes, but it's important to differentiate between making mistakes and things not working. As a coach, you should make decisions based on solid reasons. If they don't work, it doesn't mean they were wrong. Maybe the execution wasn't right. This is an important element in evaluating your performance.

But, what if you do mess up? And what if it costs you a game? I watched a game this past season that was for the Nor-Cal championship, one game away from the state title. It involved two outstanding teams and two outstanding coaches. The score was tied with ten seconds to go and the coach of one of the teams called time-out. The only problem was: he didn't have any left. Technical foul. Ball game. How does a coach deal with something like that? I believe honesty is the best policy. Admit it. Acknowledge it to your players. Let them know that you take full responsibility in the error. This will show them that you have confidence in yourself as a person and coach and that you are not above making mistakes. Also, share with them your reasoning for your decision so they know how it came about. It happens to everyone. The more prepared you become, the less often it should happen.

I read the next day that the coach did take responsibility for the time-out call, explained his thought process and apologized to his team. The players then rallied behind their coach and let him know that he was the only reason they had gone that far in the first place.

Scheduling Pre-season Games

This may be the job of the athletic director of your school, but I suggest that every coach should schedule his own games. So what do you look for when you schedule games? I know coaches who handpick their schedule so thoroughly that they almost guarantee an outstanding record, but for what? I, too, handpick my schedule but I try to balance the schedule with six or seven very difficult games, games that we have very little chance of winning. Playing such strong opposition does a lot for your team. It exposes your weaknesses and shows you what you need to work on. It also shows you a level that you can aspire to. I schedule six or seven smaller schools as well that will be similar to our league opponents which should give us a good picture of how we're progressing. To me, the most important thing is scheduling games with teams that will help you improve. It's definitely not about wins and losses.

Running up the Score or Having the Score Run Up

I have been accused of running up the score. Usually, it was by an opposing team parent who doesn't understand basketball who was just looking at the score. Scores can be misleading. Just because one team is getting blown off the court doesn't mean the other team is running it up. My players know that what is most important to me is effort—regardless of the score. People may see that my team is way ahead and working as hard as they can and take that the wrong way. I know I would hate to see the other team go easy on me just because they were far ahead. I believe that is showing disrespect for your opponent and the sport.

Yes, there are things you should do in a lopsided game. Pull off your press. I know back in 1991, very seldom did I press beyond the first quarter. We typically would pull out to a big lead right away and, at times, would have a twenty point lead five minutes into the game. Regardless of how big the margin became, I still pressed until the end of the quarter. This is not running up the score. We needed to work on that part of our game. We needed to get ready for future opponents who would be much tougher. I believe the problem begins in continuing to press after the quarter and after you already have a big lead and control of the game.

Another thing you should do is limit the minutes of your starters. That season in '91, I used preset substitutions at specific times in each game to guarantee that everyone played a lot. It worked very well.

If you are playing an especially weak opponent, you may even look to stop fast-breaking. I know I want my players to play as hard as they can every time they step on the floor and I would only force them to slow down if the other team was totally out-manned or had given up. I don't want to embarrass anyone, but I don't want my players to become lazy either. If you do this, make sure your team knows why and use the occasion to work on your half-court offense.

Awards

Awards have become somewhat controversial at our school. The "anti" point of view is that awards single out the individual and that is something that we don't want to encourage. Well, if that was all we were doing at our award ceremonies, then I would tend to agree with that statement; however, our awards banquets are much more than that. We honor our teams with an evening that consists of a sharing of the many memories of the season, a personal reflection of each player and what he meant to his teammates and coach, and a gift (usually a team shirt) to each player. The only individual awards given out are plaques that are voted on by the members of the teams themselves. This ceremony isn't about singling out individuals. It is a time to appreciate, acknowledge, and reflect upon the contributions of our teams and to thank them one last time for their effort and sportsmanship. It really is a great way to finish the season.

Choosing Captains

I have tried a little bit of everything when it comes to choosing captains. I have picked the same player(s) for the entire season, I have appointed different captains before each game, and one season (in baseball), I went the entire year without having any captains. It comes down to personnel.

What to look for,: In my mind, a captain has to be someone other players look up to. He is a player (usually an upperclassman) respected not only for his skill on the court or field, but also for his outstanding work ethic. He is a leader and a positive role model to his teammates. A coach needs to know that his captain(s) will set a good example of how to carry oneself. What does it say about your team if your captain(s) is acting up in class, showing up late to practice, or getting into some other kind of trouble outside of school?

Make sure you choose wisely, and don't make it an election. Your players may not be considering all the criteria that should go into this selection. They may choose the best or most popular player without thinking about the other traits needed, and that may lead to problems for your team down the road.

Officials, Referees, and Umpires

In organized sports, referees or officials play in integral role. You can't play the game without them. They are there to keep control of the contest.

I have built up a solid rapport with most of the officials in our area. I am a vocal coach and can be pretty animated on the sidelines on occasion, but I'm always respectful of the officials. They have a job to do just as I do. If they know you aren't trying to show them up, you will generally always get a fair shake. I expect officials to be on time, call a game consistently, hustle, and be in the right position to make the call. If they do those things, they'll never have a problem with me. As a coach, it is your responsibility to make sure your players are respectful of the officials as well. Talking back to them or disputing a call is unacceptable. If you are modeling the right behavior, it should be easy for your players to follow.

Stretching

It seems the more we find out about stretching, the more controversial it becomes. Everyone seems to have his own point of view:

> Stretching is vital to your performance,
> stretching is overrated,
> run before you stretch,
> stretch before you run,

hold the stretch for 30 seconds,
hold it for a minute, and
just hold it until you feel it's a good stretch

are just some of the conflicting views regarding this aspect of sports.

I know we don't stretch a lot and in all of my years as a coach, I haven't had one player go down with a pulled muscle let alone a torn one.

I do feel , though, as I think most coaches and trainers do, that the most important time to stretch is after the activity. This not only discourages next day muscle stiffness, but it acts as a preparation for your next workout. In *Body, Mind, and Spirit*, John Douillard, a former professional triathlete, writes,

> If waste products are completely removed from the muscles after each workout, the body can spend more time on rejuvenation, repair, and increasing performance levels during subsequent workouts.

If you do decide to implement a stretching routine for your players, whether it's before, after, or both, I suggest that you put together a program that works the entire body (at least the major muscle groups) and one that has a rhythm that is easy to remember and follow. In the book *Coaching Basketball*, Charles Brock, the head basketball coach at Drew University, has outlined his stretching program that he has had a lot of success with. Their practice begins and ends with these exercises which take fifteen minutes:

I. Jog around the court for two and one-half minutes. This increases the viscosity of the muscles and tendons, which is what we are working on. It also allows the players to "shoot the breeze," which we don't allow while stretching.

II. Sit in four lines, with the captains facing the group.
1. Hamstrings: Legs straight and together, knees locked, toes pointed to forehead.
   a. Reach down and grab leg or foot as far as possible and hold for five seconds. Repeat.
   b. Isolate. Spread legs apart and reach right hand to left leg, hold for five seconds. Left to right, hold for five seconds. Repeat.
2. Groin: "Butterflies." Put soles of feet together, pull in to body with hands, and push down on knee or calves with elbows.
3. Gluteals: "Butt." Bend left knee and cross over right knee, pull knee to the chest, hold for five seconds. Cross right over left and pull in and hold for five seconds. Repeat.
4. Lower back: Pull knees to chest. Roll back and forth, arching back.
5. Upper back and neck: Raise feet overhead and touch ground behind head. Expel air from lungs. Bring legs back and hold six inches off the ground for 15 to 20 seconds; legs straight.
6. Abdominal: Roll over on stomach and push up with arms, arching back, twist side to side.
7. Quadriceps: Kneel and lean back and try to touch the head to the ground. Always support with hands behind.

III. Standing
1. Groin: (Note: We work on this area of the body twice.) Legs spread wide, point left foot to the left; lean in that direction, right leg should be straight and right foot perpendicular to left. Reverse and repeat.
2. Sides: Latissimus dorsi. Interlock fingers and reach straight up (palms facing up). Bend side to side.

3. Ankle walks: Walk the length of the floor, up and back. Stretch ankle ligaments.

    a. length: heel to tips of toes

    b. length: tips of toes to heel

    c. length: outside of foot, roll in

    d. length: inside of foot, roll out

IV. Against the wall.

    1. Quadriceps. (Note: We also work on this area twice.) Grab the instep of the foot and pull to butt. Pull back with upper body upright, support with the other hand on the wall.

    2. Achilles: Lean straight against the wall on both hands. Push back one foot at a time; foot must be pointed straight ahead, heel down on floor. Stretch with knees straight and bent slightly.

V. Four lines.

    1. Easy jog up and back.

    2. Trotter step: Up and back, push off back foot and stretch out, at a slow to medium pace.

    3. Strider step: Up and back, push off back foot and stretch out, at a slow to medium pace.

    4. Spring: Up and back twice. All-out sprint.

These exercises have never taken longer than 15 minutes. The players are physically and mentally prepared to work.

Working With Weights

One of the biggest changes in the sports world in the last decade is the use of weight training as a method to enhance one's ability. It wasn't too long ago that so-called fitness experts were cautioning athletes about lifting weights because of the fear of becoming too bulky and losing flexibility. Now, with superior knowledge, technique, and equipment, trainers are strongly encouraging athletes to hit the weight room to not only gain an edge individually but also to keep up with the competition.

I train with weights and I've seen firsthand how they help one's performance. It just makes sense that if you become bigger, stronger, faster, and jump higher, that these attributes will help you to succeed in your sport.

My word of caution would be regarding when to start. I think when one reaches 13 or 14 is a good time to begin resistance training with just body-weight exercises such as push-ups, pull-ups, bar-dips, and sit-ups. These exercises are excellent for building a foundation to work from.

At around age 15, I would start to add free weights and machines. Definitely not any earlier. By this time, your body should already be built up a little and ready to take the next step.

I would also recommend to your athletes to make sure they get proper instruction on technique. It guarantees that they will be safe and they'll get better results.

Finally, a reminder. Good nutrition goes hand-in-hand with weight training. You need to incorporate both to get the most out of your efforts.

Treating Injuries

I have been very fortunate over the years with regard to injuries to my players. Very seldom have any of my players missed a practice, let alone a game, due to an injury. Part of the reason for our good health is, I believe, great conditioning and practicing in a fundamentally correct way. However, if someone on your team does get hurt, quick action may prevent the injury from becoming worse. The following is the procedure most coaches follow: When an injury occurs, quickly R.I.C.E. it.

R-rest: As soon as pain is felt, stop the activity immediately. Stay off the injured area as much as possible. By resting the area, tissues are allowed to begin healing themselves. Resting the area right away will often allow return to sports activity much sooner.

I-ice: Ice the injured body part for the first 24-72 hours. "Real" ice (crushed or cubed) works best, as it will conform well to the body part. Keep the ice on for 20 minutes at a time. Initially, ice at least once an hour. Never leave ice on longer than 20 minutes. After 20 minutes, the body thinks it is being frostbitten and sends lots of blood rushing to the area defeating the purpose of icing in the first place.

C-compression: Compression helps limit swelling which, if left uncontrolled, could lengthen the healing time. Keep a compression dressing (Ace wrap) around the body part. This should be wrapped snugly, but there should never be numbness, blueness, or coldness of the injured body part.

E-elevation: Elevating the injured leg or arm above the heart level helps to drain excess fluid from the injured area. Elevate the injured area on pillows for the first 24-72 hours. Continue to elevate even while sleeping.

"Unfortunately, the body always overcompensates and sends way too much blood into the area near the injury. So, by allowing all of this blood to enter the area, the injury becomes much worse.

When ice is applied, the blood vessels carrying this blood constrict, making it more difficult for this unhealthy extra blood to reach the area; therefore, any time there is a recent injury (within 72 hours), ice is the appropriate choice. Ice should also be used any time there is swelling or potential swelling. Injuries will respond well to ice when swelling is involved.

Heat on the other hand dilates the blood vessels bringing more blood into the area. Heat should be used only when more blood is wanted in the area, such as to warm up an old muscle strain before running. Heat can also be used to relax a muscle. As blood comes into the area, the muscle warms up and relaxes. Never use heat on a recent injury.

Non-traditional Treatment—Rhythmical Massage

Now this wouldn't be a Waldorf book if I didn't mention an alternative to the "normal" procedure. My good friend Jaimen McMillan, who is a movement educator and director of the Spatial Dynamics Institute, has vast experience in treating injuries by non-traditional means. One of his treatments is rhythmical massage. He and his S.D.I. colleague Maureen Foley have helped many people—including top-level athletes—by using this technique instead of the R.I.C.E. method.

I have observed Jaimen using this procedure with excellent results on a friend of mine who had hurt his knee in a game called Space Ball. Maureen also shares an experience of a gymnast who was injured at the U.S. training center in Colorado Springs and had spectacular results as my friend did with this procedure. Maureen writes:

> Jaimen and I were in Colorado holding a clinic on treatment of injuries when one young man sprained his ankle. He was taken off the floor to have ice applied to his injury. I walked over to see how he was doing and noticed his

ankle was already as big as a grapefruit even though he was icing and elevating it. I offered him an approach to reduce the swelling without the ice. He was open to it, so I started to massage the area surrounding the injury. At the time of the accident, the gymnast thought he might be out for the season. Yet, with the help of the massage work he was actually able to get back out on the floor the very next day without any swelling.

The following are tips that Maureen recommends when using rhythmical massage:

1. Do not work on the soft tissue that is injured, only on the area surrounding it.

2. Draw the fluid away from the injured tissue towards the closest joint. If you cannot apply this technique immediately, start as soon as possible.

3. Perform this procedure once every hour for the first two days, then morning, noon and evening until the swelling is gone, range of motion and stability have returned, and pain and tightness have subsided.

One final word: never diagnose an injury yourself; and make sure the player's parents are notified. Always have your injured players consult a medical professional and fill out an accident report. You can never be too careful.

Coaches, Parents, and Players

Parenting and coaching are similar in many ways. They are two of the most important professions in the world. Both play a vital role in how a child will view sports, and both play strong roles in modeling proper behavior in all aspects of life from sportsmanship and self-esteem, to dealing with adversity and despair. There's a nice poem from an unknown author that speaks to these virtues. It's entitled "A Parent Talks to a Child Before the First Game."

> This is your first game, my child. I hope you win.
> I hope you win for your sake, not mine.
> Because winning's nice.
> It's a good feeling.
> Like the whole world is yours.
> But, it passes, this feeling.
> And what lasts is what you've learned.
>
> And what you learn about is life.
> That's what sports is all about. Life.
> The whole thing is played out in an afternoon.
> The happiness of life.
> The joys.
> The heartbreaks.
>
> There's no telling what'll turn up.
> There's no telling whether they'll toss you out in the
>   first five minutes or whether you'll stay for the
>   long haul.
>
> There's no telling how you'll do.
> You might be a hero or you might be absolutely nothing.
> There's just no telling.
> Too much depends on chance.
> On how the ball bounces.
>
> I'm not talking about the game, my child.
> I'm talking about life.

But, it's life that the game is all about.
Just as I said.

Because every game is life.
And life is a game.
A serious game
Dead serious.

But, that's what you do with serious things.
You do your best.
You take what comes.
You take what comes
And you run with it.

Winning is fun.
Sure.
But winning is not the point.

Wanting to win is the point.
Not giving up is the point.
Never being satisfied with what you've done is the
point.
Never letting up is the point.
Never letting anyone down is the point.

Play to win.
Sure.
But lose like a champion.
Because it's not winning that counts.
What counts is trying.

When I think of the parents' role at my school, I think of the
tremendous support I have received. I am very fortunate to be in

a community where the parent body is so committed to their children's education. It's a wonderful feeling to know that the parents of your players have trust in your workings with their children and support you in the job you are doing. I know from my coaching friends around town, though, this unfortunately isn't always the case. A lot of coaches get out of the profession entirely because of the pressure of angry parents complaining about their child's lack of playing time. I'm sure it's hard to sit and watch your son or daughter not play, but parents can deal with this situation in a healthy way. We recently had a sport psychologist from the University of California, Davis come in to a meeting of parents, players, and coaches where he spoke about this very thing. He had some very solid tips for parents and their working with coaches and their children. Here are some of Dr. Paul Salitsky's comments:

Learn what your child's goals are first.
What do they want from their sport?
Who are they there to please?

Have realistic expectations for yourself and your child.
A lot of time and effort is required for a skilled performance.

Understand that coaching is a high stress job—that coaches are human and they're going to make mistakes. How would you like it if your child's coach came to your place of work and started telling you how to do your job?

Definitely no interference during competition.
That means do not approach the coach with a concern or issue at least twenty minutes before, during, and twenty minutes following a game. (I personally believe it should be longer. D.S.)
Try not to get too emotionally involved.

Often it is the parents' response to the athletic event that determines the type of experience the player will have—joy or misery.

Finally, if you can say that your child's team is organized, safe, and fun, and your child developingskills, is enjoying his sport experience, and is happy to be part of the team, aren't these the things that really matter? I believe so.

Questionnaire

Another tool the coach can use to evaluate coaching success is to have the players fill out a questionnaire regarding your program. You should probably put together questions that are appropriate for your own circumstances. This is one I have used.

1. How did you like practices?

2. What was your favorite part? Why?

3. What was your least favorite part? Why?

4. What would you have liked to have done differently at practice? Why?

5. How did you like the atmosphere at practice? Could it have been better?

6. What are you looking for in you team experience?

7. What's your favorite memory of the season?

8. How did you like our pregame preparation?

9. Are there any negative experiences in one of our games that you would like to share?

10. Are there any positive experiences in one of our games that you would like to share?

11. Did you achieve any or all of your goals that you set this season? Which ones? Why? Why not?

12. My goal as a coach is to make your team experience the most special you have ever had. Was it? How come? Why not?

Waves' Kai Schneider scores again.

CHAPTER 7

THE VIRTUES OF SPORT

> *You are what your deep, driving desire is.*
> *As your desire is, so is your will.*
> *As your will is, so is your deed.*
> *As your deed is, so is your destiny.*

> — Brihadaranyaka Upanishad IV.4.5

In *Games, Gymnastics, Sports in Child Development*, Kischnick asks the question, "Has sport given them (them being the generation of the 30-40 year olds which at the moment are at the height of their personal creative activity) anything which at a later age might mature into something significant?" He goes on further to say that, "Youth brings along a youthful disposition. Youngsters are open to anything which is connected with the will. For them movement is a welcome means to untie will and morality." Kischnick also adds, "Present day youth have been called to introduce a new spiritual age. Also they want to experience the spirit, even in their limbs they need physical exercise like no other generation before them, but are only able to start on this if in them devotion and enthusiasm are awakened."

I would like to respond to these statements and the question. In very few arenas other than sports, I believe, can students be so passionate about what they're doing. Because of this passion, sports gives them the opportunity for that devotion and enthusiasm to be awakened. It also creates an avenue for learning life-long lessons, such as goal setting, commitment, time management, camaraderie, discipline, work ethic, and so forth. The list goes on and on, and nowhere else, too, can teachers have the opportunity to get as close to students as through sports. I'm saddened when I hear at my school, "There's too much emphasis on sports." I hear people say that athletes' lives are out of balance and that sports are taking up too much of their time. I hear people say that "It's just a game." These people say that our athletes are dedicating their lives to sports. I see it the other way around. Our athletes are dedicating their sport to their lives. By approaching their training in a certain way, they are setting the groundwork for being successful, passionate, and happy in whatever path of life they choose to pursue. Yes, basketball is just a game. Volleyball is just a game. But that's not the issue. The game or sport is the vehicle that coaches can use to instill so many important traits and virtues. And that leads me to Kischnik's question: Has sport given the 30-40 year olds anything which at a later age might mature into something significant? My answer is: absolutely. As well as developing those qualities I just mentioned above, sports also give coaches an incredible opportunity to reach young people. What can be more significant than being a positive role model and making a difference in someone's life? Helping to instill these virtues in my players is my proudest accomplishment.

Friendship and Community

I have many memories that I will cherish forever. Each team every year has given me so much. I think of all the graduation ceremonies where my players have acknowledged with such emotion the role that I have played in their lives. It brings tears to my eyes every time. In no other vocation that I know of could I be a part of such mutual love and admiration.

I have developed so many close relationships with my players through the years. It's probably my greatest joy. It makes me very proud to see all of my players come back to our campus to visit, or show up at my practice and want to help out. Our sports program has created the opportunity for our alumni athletes to give something back to the school and has given me an arena to establish lifelong friends.

Balance

I totally disagree with people who say that our student/athletes are out of balance with the rest of their education. We practice four days a week, two hours a day. That's it. We don't have off season conditioning programs. We don't have year-round sport specialization. We don't have mandatory weight training programs. We don't even have a weight room. People perceive that our sports program is out of balance because we get so much energy from it. It comes back to passion again. The athletes are very passionate about their sports and take a great sense of pride in participation at their highest level. This doesn't mean that they drop everything else. They are still outstanding students, artists, musicians, and much more.

Self-esteem

> *Our deepest fear*
> *is not that we are inadequate.*
> *Our deepest fear is that we are*
> *powerful beyond measure.*
> *It is our light, not our darkness,*
> *that most frightens us.*
> *We ask ourselves*
> *who am I to be brilliant,*
> *gorgeous, talented, fabulous?*
> *Actually, who are you not to be?*
> *You are a child of God.*
> *Your playing small doesn't serve the world.*
> *There's nothing enlightened about shrinking*

so that other people
won't feel insecure around you.
We were all meant to shine
As children do.
We were born to make manifest
the glory of God
that is within us.
It's not just in some of us;
It's in Everyone!
And as we let our own light shine,
we unconsciously give other people
permission to do the same.
As we are liberated from our own fear,
our presence automatically liberates others!

Nelson Mandela
Inaugural speech, 1994
South Africa

Until now, I have just written about what the vehicle of sports has given to our students. I would like to expand on that and describe what it has given to our school. Beyond the extraordinary publicity (numerous feature articles in local papers every year, television spots about our program and athletes), beyond the increased enrollment, the biggest thing that our sports program has given to our school is pride. When I first came here, the students were embarrassed to say they were from Waldorf. Whenever we visited another school, we always heard, "What's a Waldorf?" We were laughed at, made fun of, and usually whipped. Our mascot became the "Waves" in 1988, and when we started to have a little success, all of our athletes wanted to be called the "The Waves." We put it on our uniforms. We were disassociating ourselves from Waldorf. I have to admit it was nice to know that no one was saying "What's a Waldorf?" anymore.

They were saying "Those guys are the Waves and they can play!" But something changed recently. I think it's mostly because we are respected throughout the community now as an outstanding sports program. Everyone knows we can play. Within our school we are now welcoming our name. Our students (athletes and non-athletes) can say with pride that we go to Waldorf and the community will not laugh. They now say, "Oh, I've heard of you guys. You're the small school that beats all the big schools."

Coach LaMere reviews game strategy before the contest begins.

Looking for a pitch to drive.

CHAPTER 8

ATHLETES AND PARENTS SPEAK

Expectations
Jud Blatchford, Class of '87
When I was younger, what I wanted to do most in life was to become a professional baseball player. It has always been my favorite sport and the one I spent the most time practicing. Because we lived in China for my 5th and 6th grade years, there was no Little League for me to play, so when we moved to Sacramento for 7th grade, I was very excited to finally play organized competitive baseball. One of my classmates in 8th grade was on my Little League team also. When my other teammates asked me where I was going to go to high school, nobody really knew about Waldorf, so it seemed that I was going to be missing out on a higher level of ball that all of them were going to play at high schools like Del Campo, San Juan, and El Camino. Before my freshman year, that was the one real concern I had and the only reason I had any doubt about attending Waldorf.

My freshman year, I didn't play on the soccer or basketball teams because I was a little intimidated by how good the upper classmen were and I didn't think I could play with them, plus I just wanted to play baseball. I was happy that Mr. Alsop was going to coach the team because I knew he was a baseball fan and was playing on an adult team. When he announced after a week or so that he wasn't going to coach, I was really disappointed, not knowing what to expect from "Mr. Stark's brother." When Dean arrived and held our first team meeting, I knew we were better off now and was really excited for the season to start. Playing as a freshman was a real thrill and to be named co-MVP with Ryan Adamson was something I was very surprised by. I was very glad to be playing at Waldorf and relieved that I could play and make a good contribution and not have to worry about all the talent at a public school after all. The only disappointments were that we could only practice four days a week, and occasionally I had to miss a practice because of a class field trip.

Something I really liked about Waldorf was that you got to know your teammates in many other ways besides on the field or court. To get to know them through other classes, field trips, camping trips, and work week was really neat; I think it helped our competition because we were playing with our best friends.

Well I did get the desire to compete in other sports eventually and ended up playing soccer and basketball as well as baseball in my sophomore, junior, and senior years. The sports at Waldorf became a huge part of my whole high school experience. And I also got a chance to compete with and against some of my old Little League friends in the summers in Senior League baseball and found out that I wasn't missing much in High School baseball after all. I continued to play all three sports through my senior year and had a lot of fun. It is ironic because if I had gone to a public school, I'm sure I would never have been encouraged to even go out for soccer or basketball, which I had a lot of fun playing even though they weren't my #1 sport. Even coming out of a small Division 5 school, I managed to join a Division 1 university baseball team, and actually got to play—one of the most satisfying things I've done.

Now I'm teaching at a large public school in Colorado and oddly enough coaching their varsity baseball team. It has been a real eye-opener for me. There have been a lot of good times in my three seasons of coaching at a public school, but a lot of frustration that I didn't anticipate. It is difficult to determine if these frustrations are truly a difference in large public as opposed to small private schools, or whether they are just a matter of the circumstances I happen to be in, or simply how times have changed in general. At Waldorf the players regarded Dean with the utmost respect, and I don't recall there ever being any parent interference. So far in coaching, I have encountered many players who feel they know it all, who don't have a good work ethic and who play for themselves instead of for the team. I have had parents call me to tell me where their son should play and what spot in the batting order he should hit in, who tell me that their son on the bench is better than the player starting ahead of him. I have been threatened to be sued because of cutting a player. The list goes on.

It very well may be a combination of a few factors. Maybe the parents at Waldorf don't know a sport in as much depth as some do in public school, maybe they trust that the coach is already trying to do what's right for their children, maybe they realize that what position their son plays is an insignificant detail in the large picture of their child's development. It is hard to say for sure. I feel that many parents I have encountered in public school look at their child through rose colored glasses and have very unrealistic expectations/opinions in regard to their son's talent. Many of the players I have coached also have unrealistic views of their own ability.

As I said at the start, I have also had many good times coaching. One of the benefits of coaching at a large school is that the talent pool from a student population of 1,800 is generally greater than from a population of just over 100. And to compete against other large schools will produce some good games to be involved in from a standpoint of watching good players play.

All things considered however, I think I would rather be in a Waldorf type setting where I could see my players every day in settings other than on the field and develop a close relationship with them. They would be able to see better how much I care for them and in return would give me their best effort on the field. At Waldorf, I will always remember what Dean did for his players—like coming to my house after I broke my nose to see if I was getting better. Because I respected him so much I always gave him my best effort.

The Inner Process of Hoops
Colin Poer, Class of '91
As in the case of many other players, my basketball career began on a cracked blacktop with sagging nine-foot rims. The school court was nestled between classrooms and a green cow pasture and was surrounded by trees that towered over the court, often serving as shot blockers to long range shots. I have many memories of that court—playing in the rain with my best friend, wearing garbage bags, and carefully stepping through the cow pasture to rescue a basketball. We even had a few high school basketball practices on that court when there were gym rental complications. Now that court is gone because of school growth, but the memories of the humble beginnings of the Sacramento Waldorf basketball program live on.

There are many unique experiences that have made my athletic career at Waldorf memorable. From the 3:00 varsity games at the rented gym with as many as four or five fans in attendance, to playing cello with the other four starters in the high school orchestra cello section, from the inspirational pre-game talks in gymnasium storage closets to grueling one-on-one games with my coach—these experiences are more than just nostalgia; they taught me, guided me, balanced me, and formed me.

The Waldorf high school experience was an integral part of my growth and development both as a person and a basketball player. I was fortunate to attend a school which recognized that a charcoal still life drawing, bowing a minuet, writing an essay, and throwing down a dunk were equally important in creating balance in students. Deeply experiencing these different aspects of education has allowed me to honor and value the multiplicity of the human soul. In college, both my academic and athletic experiences taught me that balance is not always the outcome of a so-called liberal arts education. I feel that my experiences in high school allowed me the freedom to explore and develop passions for diverse areas from art to science, from philosophy to history.

The small school artistic and academic environment did not mean that athletics were merely recreational. The athletic program is an integral part of the high school experience at Waldorf. I was fortunate to be a part of the humble beginnings of that success.

Waves Basketball starting five also play cello in the school orchestra.

When I began playing, our team success and our team image had no relationship. Limited budgets and a no-frills program left us players with tight polyester shorts, peeling numbers, and no warm-ups. The public school teams we played would stream out onto the court in a single file wearing flashy matching outfits, while we "Waldorfians" would come out in our dysfunctional apparel. Our appearance would often summon sneers and laughs from opponents. But, when they were trailing at half-time, the public schools would find a new respect. Our team was an example of a now dying philosophy—a philosophy that was core to our coach Dean Stark's approach to the game and life: it's not what's outside, but what's inside that counts the most. It was not our sometimes disorganized appearance that characterized our team, but rather the discipline, dedication, teamwork, and fire in our hearts that fueled our success.

Fans often remarked how well we played together as a team. Knowing some of my teammates since grade school definitely helped our cohesiveness, but it's more than just knowing each other that created this team chemistry. The Waldorf philosophy encouraged a family-like class environment where respect and trust were developed among us. It was out of this trust and confidence in each other that we developed our strong unity. Both the class and team experiences have taught me that it is the substance of the relationships between people, the emotions, struggles and triumphs, that are more important than the wins and losses, the outcome. It was the process of growing as a team that I admire and cherish the most now. Both the teachers and Coach Stark recognized that it is the quality of the process that is more important than the outcome. This simple but sacred truth has lived on in me as a gift that I strive to follow. I feel that it was this understanding that allowed us to achieve our success and to grow as a team. Of course, the success and team character we developed were the fruits of Dean's positive attitude, commitment, and hard work.

We all respected, trusted, and admired Dean because he respected us. I remember as a sophomore having a bad practice and out of frustration deciding to give up trying hard. Dean challenged me not to quit and to stay with it. He encouraged me to strive through those times, to believe in myself and the team. Through my high school and college basketball career, I have had many important conversations with Dean. It is his openness, respect, and trust that creates the foundations for the many close relationships he has with his players. Unlike many coaches, Dean was and still is an example of what he challenged us to be: dedicated, determined, disciplined, and present. When he challenged us to not miss a practice or not to give up when we were down, we knew that he spoke out of his truth and out of his own experience. Amazingly enough, during my junior and senior year, almost everyone on the team did not miss one game or one practice. We wanted to give 100% because we knew he would give everything he had.

My college basketball experiences made me realize how rare and important my athletic experience at Waldorf was. The truths that I learned and lived there inspired me to coach high school basketball. I feel it is important that young people have positive, challenging experiences that inspire them to look within themselves and ask: who am I? and can I do this? I am thankful to Dean Stark, my teachers, and the Waldorf school for supporting and allowing me to ask these questions.

Self-expression
Andy Goncalves, Class of '91
My memories and experiences of playing basketball at the Sacramento Waldorf School are yet to be equaled. The lasting friendships that were developed with both teammates and coach, as well as the joy of expressing myself athletically are the prima-

ry reasons for this. However, the entire educational process at Waldorf was significant in making my experience a unique one.

For me, the heart of my education at Waldorf was self-expression. Whether this expression was athletic, artistic, or simply expressing my frustration at having to do homework, teachers and coaches always had an open ear. This freedom and encouragement to be open and honest was not limited to the school day; it carried over into all school-related activities, sports included.

During basketball practices, we would have so much fun. Had the coach not finished the practices with running for conditioning purposes, I am not at all convinced that we would have gone home. Aside from simply loving the game, the freedom to enjoy and express ourselves within the context of practices was why it was so much fun. When I compare this to what I experienced at college, it holds true. Nearly everyone at college dreaded practices because they were so rigid and controlled. They were a chore to be endured in order to play in the games. This was such a contrast to my Waldorf experience. It was a little disheartening to see so many people who loved the game of basketball having so little fun playing it.

Mutual respect between the players and the coach was also a contributing factor in my experience being a positive one. I looked at Dean as a friend first and coach second. He was a role model to me and it was very easy to respect him because of the way he treated people and lived his life. Our friendship has remained intact to this day and I'm sure will continue into the future.

A Waldorf Athletic Experience
Jeffrey Dorso, Class of '93
I was a student at the Sacramento Waldorf School from kinder-

garten through the twelfth grade. During those thirteen years, I had many wonderful experiences that I feel contributed to my growth as an individual, from my building and baking blocks in the third grade, to my symptomatology project in the twelfth grade. Of these varied experiences, there is one that I am most grateful for, and that is my athletic experience I received in high school through soccer, baseball, and in particular, basketball.

When I entered high school, I had never played baseball, was intrigued by basketball, and was an accomplished soccer player. Thus, I thought I would play soccer and try basketball. Baseball was not even on my mind. However, through my experience in both soccer and basketball, I decided (and was encouraged) to try baseball. I played the entire season, and found that baseball was not in my blood; however, this experience is one aspect of the positive side of atheletics in a Waldorf environment. I was given a chance to participate on a team—in a sport I had never played—and see if I enjoyed it. In many other situations, I would never have had that experience. I was encouraged to play every sport in 9th Grade, and for that I am forever grateful. I learned much about myself and others from my participation in three different sports. This participation in a variety of sports greatly complemented my diverse curriculum. I now want to shift your focus to that which I cherish most from my years at Waldorf, my high school basketball experience.

For me, my basketball experience at Waldorf represented everything that education and personal developement is all about. My basketball experience started with my J.V. team's losing every game during my first year. By the end of my high school basketball experience, I was fortunate enough to play for the Section championship twice and go to three straight play-off appearances— but when I remember the most rewarding and enjoyable part of playing basketball, I don't think of all the victories or playing in huge venues for the Section championship. I remember practicing with my teammates. We loved practice. Basketball was, in a sense, almost secondary. The beauty of practice was the pursuit of perfection in a common goal, where every individual on the team played a keystone role. While the talent level of the basketball team, or any Sacramento Waldorf team for that matter, covered a broad range, everyone played an equal role in the success of our team. The least talented basketball player on the team was just as crucial as the most talented player, because what made our basketball team click was our united striving for perfection. This awareness is an aspect that is unique to Waldorf athletics; it allowed us to separate ourselves and defeat teams from larger high schools that had more basketball talent. The goal of perfection was sought after through the many intangibles that each player brought, along with effort and attitude. The importance of every individual, as well as not being afraid to put everything one has into achieving our goal, was something everyone learned in large part through the guidance of our coach, Dean Stark, who made this environment possible. Much the same as the Waldorf curriculum sets out to develop a love for knowledge within the child, so we were placed in a position to appreciate and love the hard work that it takes to be successful in any medium, which in this case was basketball.

Giving 100%

Jayan Berman, Class of '96

When I think about Waldorf basketball, I find myself reflecting on the past; I see myself as a freshman submerged in the sport. I remember carrying the basketball everywhere I went. My thoughts dwelt constantly on the game. When I was a sophomore and the season approached, I was ready. My opportunity finally arrived and I stepped forward to embrace it.

Through four years of high school, I learned about giving the sport everything I had every time I played, whether I was in practice or in a game. In my small school, there were only a few of us able to participate and each of us needed to show up willing to give 100% of ourselves every day. I learned that if I gave anything less than all—less than 100%—I would later feel a deep regret. It became essential for me to leave everything—all of my energy and all of my hustle—on the gym floor.

At first, I thought that this understanding of how important it was to always give my best effort was spontaneously rising up inside me. As I matured a little, I realized that my own understanding and recognition was a result of some kind of Waldorf tradition that had always existed. This tradition, this putting forth one's whole heart and soul existed before I ever held a basketball.

It has occurred to me that this so-called "tradition" has grown in time side by side with Waldorf education. In my school, I have no doubt that it was Dean Stark who took this willingness on the part of Waldorf students and nurtured it into a truly healthy and enriching environment.

The Fire of the Will
Dylan Hickey, Class of '98
Each breath was like a thousand needles piercing my lungs as I leaned against the paddle wall behind the baseline. My legs quivered with exhaustion and all I could see were the exploding lights around my dizzying head. Then those five dreaded words echoed through my world with painful clarity: "Eight line drill, ready, go!!" Without a second thought, I turned around and pushed myself past the eleventh set of eight lines. Dean warned us that we would miss times like those after we graduated—miss

testing our bodies and our will—and if you can believe it, I miss every moment.

This is a recollection of my experience playing basketball at a Waldorf school. I realize that this recollection has very little to do with Waldorf and much more to do with its coach, Dean Stark, and his ability to create energy and passion among the players on his many Waldorf teams. In Dean's eyes, success isn't measured in wins and losses but rather in effort and heart. When I started playing for Dean as a sophomore, it became evident that fear and insecurity were no longer options in my repertoire of emotions. During a game that year, I remember feeling intense fear and hesitation in the first quarter of play. Dean immediately sensed my feelings and took me aside; he made it perfectly clear that those emotions were detrimental to my play and had no place on the court. I then sat on the bench for a few minutes and realized that he was right. In the realm of basketball, the only emotions one should feel are intensity and passion; all others cloud the purity of the sport.

Having been a lifetime Waldorf student, I had the privilege of watching previous Waldorf teams dominate the league with demoralizing ease. My childhood heroes were players from those teams. During grade school, my friends and I would go to the games religiously and root the team on. During recess the next day, we would pretend we were the players in the game and reenact our favorite highlights. Throughout junior high, we practiced continuously, fueled by the dream of someday playing basketball for Dean and Waldorf. In high school, our efforts were rewarded with the single most positive experience of our lives: playing varsity basketball and realizing a childhood dream. We saw the cycle repeat itself. Our loudest and most intense fans were the children from the middle and lower schools—insuring that passion for Waldorf basketball would not die when we graduated but continue as the next generation of dreamers filled our shoes and pushed the program further into the future.

Since Waldorf is so small, the majority of the players were, and are, not particularly gifted with tremendous athletic talent. Nevertheless, the basketball program has continually proved itself worthy of praise from the larger, better endowed schools— a direct result of the work ethic Dean has brought to the school and the program. The team has established a reputation for being one of the most intense and well-disciplined small school teams in the Sacramento area.

For the alumni, it has become tradition to tell stories of games and practices from their time to the younger players. One of the exclusive aspects of Waldorf basketball is the brotherhood that a player enters when he joins the team. Even though I have graduated and left the school, I still feel connected with the current team as well as with the many alumni who preceded me.

My time with the Waldorf basketball program has been a rewarding and integral part of my life. It presented me with the opportunity to revel in my own dreams and explore my character as a growing human being. Through the teachings of Dean, I have learned that my life can be forged into whatever I want, if only I use the fire of my will

Transformation
Dennis Klocek, Parent
My wife and I have often wondered how it is possible that children coming from the same parents and growing up in the same family could be so fundamentally different. Our three sons have given us this fact to consider many times as they were growing up. My wife and I met in art school and gave the values of art as

a way of life to our oldest son. We also seem to have given him a bias against sports by stressing the importance of art. As the boys grew up, however, the other two boys were powerfully attracted by the sports program in the high school. While both of them play instruments and sing and draw and paint, they also have strong bodies and a keen sense of wanting to test themselves. At first, my wife and I were skeptical and concerned that they would become too competitive. This feeling vanished for me when I saw my son in a game for the first time. Every time someone passed him the basketball, he froze and looked around in panic to pass the ball to someone else. I saw fear in his eyes and a sense of failure on his face. I realized that the running and intense practice he was getting set the stage for a healthy physical body, and that the composure needed to dribble a ball in the face of a defender, or the courage it took to drive down the center of a mass of defenders, were essential to his development as a whole person. As the years went by and he matured into a commanding presence on his team, I saw that his lessons on the court were a precise and economical education in leadership and perseverance. My wife and I gradually became boosters for the team and took great delight seeing our son dominate the backboards over much larger opponents solely through his intensity and focus. We had seen a dreamy, evasive sleepyhead turn into a competent playmaker and team energizer. My wife also loves the fact that during basketball season, the boys are too tired after school to get cranky over chores at home or other adolescent issues. Through sports, they have a constructive, team-oriented outlet for their tremendous energies. They work harder for our family when they are working hard for their team. I know that this is not always the case when young athletes only devote themselves to their sport. In our family, however, sport, homework, art, and social activities are things which we try to keep in balance.

At the final game of our graduating senior, I thought of his development and felt gratitude for the coaches and organizers whose sacrifice and caring made his transformation possible. He is in college now and is active in rock climbing, bicycling, and writing songs at the piano. He draws better than some of his art teachers. He still is balanced and adept in many things. But we have another soccer-playing, aspiring basketball hopeful coming along. So come November, my wife and I will be at the gym rooting for the team, watching for another transformation, and thanking our stars for the dedicated coaching.

Perhaps we'll see you there.

Balance
Tom Adamson, Parent
One very important area where Waldorf excels, both in its education and in its sports programs, is summed up in one word—balance. In education, it strives to teach a balance of the whole child, not just the mind. How often have we heard that it is better to be well-rounded than one dimensional? Too much of even something good for you can be very unhealthy. In our individual lives, we seek balance because it leads to a happier, healthier existence.

This idea of balance is really the main reason my wife and I chose to keep our youngest son, Matthew, in the Waldorf educational system for his high school years. The temptation for him to transfer was the larger sports programs at other schools. We were looking at Jesuit, a private Catholic school, with a great tradition in sports and a very enthusiastic student body that supports their teams. It was obvious early on that Matt was potentially good enough in basketball to play for Jesuit. He also had a 4 handicap in golf at that time and Jesuit has an outstanding golf team each

year. My feeling at the time, however, was that Waldorf's education was more balanced, and the same could be said for its sports
program. Playing basketball at Jesuit would have been way more
intense and all-consuming with a great deal more pressure
involved. To put it more simply, I felt basketball at Waldorf
would be more fun for Matt. Only about 1% of high school basketball players end up playing on a college team. That means
99% end their careers after high school. Having fun should be a
high priority. At the same time you want it to be competitive and
challenging. Waldorf's basketball program had this balance.

I also believed at the time that if Matt worked hard on his game
and developed as a player through his high school years, his
chances of playing on the college level would be just as good out
of Waldorf as it would have been from Jesuit. There are a lot of
parents who wouldn't agree with that statement. Surely you
would be seen more readily playing on a team like Jesuit's with
its more competitive schedule and greater media coverage. My
feeling was that if you were good enough, no matter who you
played for, you would be found by college scouts. Good players
with good attitudes do not fall through the cracks.

As it turned out, Matthew proved me to be right. He had a wonderful time in his high school basketball career without getting
burned out which happens so often. He went on to play for division 1 Notre Dame University. No one from Jesuit has ever
played for Notre Dame. There was one negative aspect to his
sports career however. His golf game went to pot.

Managing a Full Schedule
Marianne Alsop, Parent
I have been fortunate enough to have two children who attended
the Waldorf School for twelve years (fourteen if you count nurs-

ery and kindergarten). Both of my children are sports enthusiasts, they have grown up with a healthy appreciation of athletics and both of them have continued this appreciation into their college years.

Their high school years were filled with most of the normal tumult that that time brings. Friends and a multitude of activities filled their lives. Because they attended a school where it was expected that they participate fully in an academic life (foreign language, mathematics, sciences, humanities, social sciences) as well as the more aesthetic classes (art, music, drama). Was it unusual that they also participated in sports? These sports were always extracurricular, meaning always after school. What about homework? Waldorf high school students rarely have fewer than several hours a day of papers to write, exams to study for— and who can forget main lesson books to finish? Add to that rehearsal time for musical instruments, eurythmy performances, and remaining on familiar terms with parents. Is this a recipe for exhaustion?

Strangely enough it isn't. Rhythm is a vital part of the Waldorf curriculum and it has always been an important part of my children's involvement with sports during their high school years. For many students at this age, physical activity is a real need. Their bodies are growing and changing; they need to experience the space they are growing into. Being on a team is also an important activity. Working together as a group, learning to listen to the coach, following directions, and concentration are magnificent tools.

Because there were only so many hours in the day, and because doing nothing was also one of their favorite pastimes, they had to organize their lives so that everything had a place of importance. Rhythm in the day, the week, and in the season became an essential part of their lives. Meals had to take place on time, and usually five to seven meals a day were the norm. The meals had to be nutritious. Our coaches set the tone here through their own example. Sleep: a minimum of six to eight hours. And time to spend with friends: as much as possible.

School work usually came first—homework taken care of during a study hall period or after dinner at night. After school practice was a wonderful time to be with "the team" and blow off steam, working hard to play well together. We were fortunate enough to have good coaches who were sensitive enough to the students' needs and allow a practice to end early if a major exam or project was due on the following day. Wednesday afternoons were always free, leaving a space to do whatever they desired.

It happened several times that a major musical competition for both choir and orchestra would fall the morning after a far away tournament game. Sleepy-eyed and with their ties somewhat askew, the students would appear, awaken, and sing and play as beautifully as they would have had they had twelve hours sleep. Amazingly, they could balance all the demands on their lives quite well. In fact both of my own children and many others have told me that being involved with sports gave them the opportunity to arrange their time in a way that would make it all work. It all had to do with rhythm. And they were happy!

As a parent, I found this to be a wonderful time and it passes very quickly. I had to be an integral part of the rhythm. Without a mom or dad readily available to cook, drive, sew, cheer, and console, it wouldn't work as well. I guess parents are the support staff of a student's life, both physically and emotionally.

Going to the games and watching your son or daughter play on the team is great—it is a lot of fun. Winning is nice, but after a while who really remembers the score? What stays with you, though, is that you got to be there at that very special time, just before they left home for college or to travel the world, and you loved them and yelled for them and acted really crazy in front of all their friends . . . and they knew it, and they didn't mind one bit!

CHAPTER 9

HOW TO BUILD A PROGRAM

The universe is my way.
Love is my law.
Peace is my shelter.
Experience is my school.
Obstacle is my lesson.
Difficulty is my stimulant.
Pain is my warning.
Work is my blessing.
Balance is my attitude.
Perfection is my destiny.

— Guillermo Tolentino

Your school has decided to start a sports program; or it has committed to improving its current one. What's the next step? I believe it starts with the coaching staff. You need to have qualified teachers to lead the way. Ideally, these people are already within the school, because they will already understand the philosophy of the school and have a built-in relationship with the students—but, don't hire your English teacher to coach the volleyball team just because she's on staff and has played the sport in high school. You need to hire the best person for the job.

One of the reasons why I believe the Sacramento Waldorf School has been so successful over the years is the outstanding coaching and consistency within the staff. I already mentioned that I've been coaching here for twelve years. We also have had the same soccer coach for eight years and the same girls' basketball coach for six seasons. The only inconsistency we have had within our department has been volleyball and softball and, consequently, these sports have been our least successful. Pursue these positions as thoroughly as you would a teaching position. It will make a huge difference.

Another vital role in establishing a sports program is the relationship between the sports department and the administration and faculty. The administration has to be in full support of the program. To make this happen, communication is a must. Probably my biggest weakness in my early years was not working with my administration. I was doing everything I knew to build a program, I was giving my all for my players, but I wasn't concerned or aware of developing a relationship with my peers. The faculty members that vocally supported the program (usually parents of my players) were my friends, and the rest I didn't have time for. Yet, I couldn't understand why everyone wasn't in my corner. I think the problem was I have always been the type of person who will get the job done by himself. I had the mentality that I didn't need anybody else, so I would just do things without going through the proper channels and the administration would be frustrated because they had no knowledge of what was going on: until they received a bill for eight dozen baseballs or a note from an angry teacher that read, "The coach has my students out of class again without any notice!" Those are things of the past, though. It has been amazing to me to see how supportive the administration can be when they are working with you in the pursuit of the same goal—to enrich the lives of the students.

By keeping everyone informed of what's going on ahead of time, one eliminates a lot of potential headaches. A couple of things that have really helped our collegial relationship run smoothly have been published early-dismissal dates and regular budget meetings. We inform our teachers before the season starts about all of the dates and times student athletes will miss class. This allows the instructors to prepare their lesson plans accordingly. I have also found that meeting periodically with the administration to make sure our financial situation stays in the black has made for good working relations and balanced budgets.

Regarding the budget, it's very important that you establish one that will allow you to be successful. That means you have to spend what it takes for quality coaches, proper equipment, uniforms, and facilities. We have no frills in our budget, but we also make sure that everything is covered sufficiently. For example, our baseball budget includes: baseballs, umpires, chalk for the fields, and transportation. We also have an allotment for equipment replacement each year. That's it. Everything on there is a must.

When it comes down to establishing your own budget, sit down with the coaches and itemize each sport. From there, meet with the administration and put it together. Do everything you can to keep the cost down but don't skimp. If a team wants anything extra (practice uniforms, jackets, and so on), we fundraise.

Just as important as the relationship of the sports department and administration is the one of the sports department and student body. At the Sacramento Waldorf School, we consistently have about 70% of the student body participating in the athletic program, but more than that has been the universal support we have received. It's not an uncommon sight to see our rented gymnasium (before our present Festival Hall/Gymnasium was completed in the winter of '97) filled with our student body and with dozens of kids from the lower grades. This school spirit has developed through the years in a number of ways. Continued success of the sports teams has instilled the tradition of excellence within our program. This fosters a loyal following of fans every year—fans who can expect sportsmanship, effort, and enthusiasm from our athletes. And the close-knit relationships we cultivate within the foundation of our school also help to bring about the unified support that we receive. It gives a definite feel of a community coming together to share our pride in our school.

Speaking of community, I feel involving your community with your sports program is a great way to establish yourself. It builds enthusiasm. Keep the alumni informed of what's happening and mail them copies of your team's schedule. Mail your schedules to local businesses as well. Take advantage of the area's newspapers to let people know what is happening at your school. We get as much publicity at our school as any other school in town. Not bad for a high school with 100 students.

Having the entire school work together towards the same goal is what it takes. You need support from the administration and faculty, the student and parent body, the community and the Booster Club to make it work. But remember, it all starts with the coaches. They need to have the courage, vision, and knowledge to make your goals and dreams come alive.

The Booster Club

With the success of the boys' basketball program it was just a matter of time until a girls' program would begin. In 1987, however, a strong nucleus of young women arrived who wanted to start a girls' basketball team. Because there had never been a team before there wasn't any money budgeted for it within the school. That's when the Waves Booster Club was formed.

The parents of several basketball players (girls and boys) met over the course of a few weeks to organize a Booster Club. First, a list of priorities was established: hire a coach for the girls' team and find a way to pay him, rent the gym, create a schedule of games (would there be anyone who wanted to play us?), pur-chase uniforms, and get the word out that basketball was now for girls as well as boys! It didn't take long. With the announcement of the first-ever barbecue for families and supporters of Sacramento Waldorf School sports, the first Booster event was launched. Everyone attending was given the opportunity to join the club for a nominal $30.00 per family per year contribution. That first event launched the non-budgeted girls' varsity basket-ball program. The girls' program became an integral part of Sacramento Waldorf High School sports. It is hard to remember that it wasn't always that way!

In subsequent years, this group has remained in the hands of a few dedicated parents. Giving hours and hours of their time, they have managed, through various fundraising activities, not only to purchase uniforms and warm-up suits, but also to have contributed to newsletters with schedules of the games for the entire school to enjoy; provided busses for the fans to get to far-away playoff games; made scholarship aid available for players to attend team camps during the summer; supported and worked with the coaches to create the best atmosphere possible for high school sports.

The Waves Booster Club has been able to make its presence felt through the continued $30.00 annual contributions of school and alumni families. Other activities include the sale of T-shirts designed with the booster logo and in our school colors, booster club pins, running the snack bar concession, and collecting admission fees to basketball games (club members may attend for $2.00 while non-members pay $4.00). Members are asked to staff the snack bar and work the admission table, and nearly everyone does this with a sense of joy in making something spe-cial possible for our children. The club has offered the parents of our school a way of being involved not only with their own children, but with all the players, at many different levels of competition.

At the end of each sports season the club hosts a special dinner at school to recognize all the players and coaches. Many photos are taken and special memories and humorous accounts are given of the past season. It is important for young people at this age to have athletic ability recognized (as well as academic, artistic and musical abilities which are an integral part of the Waldorf curriculum).

What this body does above all is create a form in which many sporting activities, which could not be fully supported by the school financially, can become reality. Realizing the importance of sports in the lives of our children, and the need for parents to be a part of that, is what keeps this group going!

As a postscript, our school recently opened its new Festival Hall, a combination gymnasium and theatre. For the first time in the history of our school, we are hosting opposing teams in our own gym. The Booster Club has played a part in making this hall a reality and its energy continues to be felt through various activities that will lead to the purchase of bleachers and scoreboards. Parents are a vital force in every school. Having those parents work together towards a common goal strengthens community in the school and can make dreams come true.

The recently completed festival hall at the Sacramento Waldorf School.
Dreams do come true.

CHAPTER 10

VIEWS FROM OTHER WALDORF PROGRAMS

Highland Hall School
Humberto Ramirez

In the fifteen years that I have been here at Highland Hall Waldorf School, I have had to adjust my approach and style to accommodate each group of students I encounter. The most consistent attitude that I have maintained is that I can convince the athletes that the particular sport they participate in is worth their time for improvement and competitive effort. I also believe that I would rather coach team sports and not individual sports because you basically have to rely on others and that is a rewarding challenge for me.

Lately, I have been attempting to follow a process that best suits me and what I would like to see in a group of players. First and foremost, any activity that I teach has to be fun. The players should enjoy any activity they participate in. My approach to making activities fun is to give the players a series of tasks in progression that they can be successful at. I have learned that drills which incorporate some form of competition have worked best. Giving my players recognition for their effort, attitude, and improvement is also a very important part of my process as a coach. They need to know and hear that I appreciate their hard work and sportsmanship.

Eventually, my hope is that players will experience a self-actualization and develop a true desire to see how good at a given sport they can be. This is when a player makes a commitment to be the best he or she can be. Involved in this area are off-season workouts, individual work on skills, self-conditioning, learning the game, and self-discipline. These are aspects of any given sport that create a championship attitude.

This process can be followed to develop life skills as well. I do not let a season of play go by without reminding players that any qualities learned during the course of a season such as sportsmanship, leadership, teamwork, and competitiveness are qualities that they can apply in any life situation outside of sports.

My coaching philosophy is to contribute to the development of a total human being with the application of these ideas: to have fun and be successful, to be recognized for the effort one gives, and to realize that they can reach their goals in life.

Green Meadow Waldorf School
Will Crane
Since the curriculum of the Waldorf School is based on an understanding of human development, it naturally arises that physical education is a vital element in aiding the children in the process of incarnation. The schools' athletic programs are, likewise, an important and integral part of the educational experience. In the physical education classes, the students are introduced to fundamentals of many sports and movement activities in a way which is age and developmentally appropriate. The opportunity to pursue some specific sports activities more deeply is supported by the after-school sports program.

Current Program

Fall I
Tennis, cross-country, basketball, volleyball, softball, and baseball are programs currently being offered to students at Green Meadow. At this point tennis is offered to 7th and 8th graders as a clinic and an intramural, co-ed activ-

ity in the spring, while the high school students (grades 10, 11, 12) play it as a co-ed, competive sport in the fall.

Fall II
Cross-country running is a new fall sport for Green Meadow. While we have not yet competed with other schools, both boys and girls (grades 10,11,12) train together with the emphasis on self-improvement and conditioning.

Winter
Basketball is still (by far) the most popular sport among our students. There are presently six teams: 7/8 Grade Boys, 7/8 Grade Girls, Varsity Boys, J.V. Boys, Varsity Girls, and J.V. Girls.

Spring
Softball is played in the spring by the girls in the high school (grades 9-12), while baseball is played by the boys. The boys are currently in a league with baseball and basketball, and we are seeking a league affiliation for the girls. This helps to promote a steady schedule and credibility within an organization outside of the Waldorf school movement.

Philosophy/Policy
We have no tryouts and make no cuts. All interested players may join and practice with the team in their age group. An attempt is made to give all players game experience and help each to develop his or her skill level in competition. Teamwork and good sportsmanship are cultivated by the example and guidance of the coach.

The decision not to allow 9th graders to participate in school sports or other extracurricular activities in the fall was made by the high school faculty in order to allow the students time, without other distractions, to meet the rigorous academic challenge of high school. All athletes are expected to maintain their academic standing, keep up with their school work, refrain from smoking and/or using drugs or alcohol at any time. Failure to do so results in suspension and possible expulsion from the team. The students sign a contract to this effect.

Administration

While administration of the athletic program is carried out by the athletic director on a day-to-day basis, an Athletic Committee oversees the program as a whole and deals more with policy changes and issues. The larger group helps to support the work of the athletic director and represents many sides of a given issue. It may also receive other delegated responsibilities and it helps with future planning and development.

Conclusion

We see the athletic programs at Green Meadow as continually developing aspects of the school. We strive to keep up with the growing needs of the student population within the limits of our budget and in a manner consistent with the educational principles of the school.

The Waldorf School of Lexington

Ralph Brooks

The Waldorf School of Lexington, in conjunction with the Massachusetts Bay Independent League, maintains a philosophy based on several principles. Accordingly, all member schools subscribe to the following in the conduct of their athletic programs:

> This league shall provide students with the opportunity for self-growth and a building of self-esteem.

Member teams and coaches shall strive to behave according to the highest levels of sportsmanship and respect. We expect that visitors will be treated with courtesy and that visiting teams will act as honored guests.

The league was founded and shall continue to exist with the purpose of offering a forum for balanced competition amongst the member schools.

We believe that each school assumes the responsibility to inform its constituency that the athletic arena is a place for friendly and spirited competition and respect for all who are part of that forum.

We believe that our athletic programs should offer a teaching environment that is understood to be consistent with the overall educational goals of each member school.

We believe that member schools have a responsibility to work together to resolve differences that will arise from time to time. We have a responsibility to one another's programs and initiatives consistent with the goals of The Massachusetts Bay Independent League.

Team Sports and Physical Education
We believe that team sports are inappropriate for children below the seventh grade but they can be confidence-builders for older students *when properly coached*. We stress sportsmanship. We start every class with a greeting and end with a handshake. It is very important that students learn to win gracefully and to lose gracefully. Self-confidence, not cockiness, is the goal. It is important to compliment the other team on a good play. Parental attitudes also can have a big impact on how children behave on the field.

Once they are in high school, students spend two hours a week in PE activities: Swimming (which includes stroke mechanics, lifesaving, water polo, and water basketball), Rock Climbing (which includes learning to belay and rappel, and to climb over-hangs), Team Sports (which include basketball, beach volleyball on an outdoor sand court, and gym hockey), Fitness and Aerobics (which includes strength training with free weights and on Nautilus equipment as well as cardiovascular work like step aerobics and cross-country running), and Ballroom Dancing (in which students learn to lead and follow while doing the waltz, tango, foxtrot, Charleston, and swing). This last block was so popular this year that the High School held a spring Ballroom Dance for students, parents, and faculty.

One of the goals of the high school program is to encourage a life-long love of physical endeavor. Our physical education curricu-lum offers activities that one can do for a lifetime.

In addition to our PE program, we also offer an after-school ath-letic program for 7th-through-12th grades. In the 1999-2000 school year, students may compete in soccer in the fall, basketball in the winter, and cross-country in the spring, playing other schools in the Boston area. The high school boys' and girls' bas-ketball teams will play an 18-game schedule in the coming year as trial members of the Massachusetts Bay Independent League and the Girls Independent League respectively. The cross-coun-try runners will be competing in weekend races all over eastern Massachusetts. High school students have the opportunity to participate in a sailing program on the Charles River during the fall and spring and fifth-through-eighth graders can participate in the ski program at Wachusett Mountain during the winter.

One highlight of the athletic program is the annual student-fac-ulty basketball game held on May Day. This fundraiser earned $700 this year for the Athletic Booster Club.

CHAPTER 11

THE ACTION PLAN—PUTTING IT ALL TOGETHER

You have your goals and quotes. The faculty, student body, and boosters are behind you. Your players are excited about the season. So, how do you put it all together? If you have followed my suggestions in the section on the coach's role with his team, you are already well on your way. Believe in this information and in yourself. Each aspect plays an important part in the success, fulfillment, and enjoyment of your season and profession.

The last missing pieces to the puzzle of successful coaching are fundamentals and conditioning. I've already written about knowledge and striving to learn as much as possible about your sport. Teaching the proper fundamentals and conditioning your team in addition to the motivating, goal-setting, and preparation is what's going to put you over the top.

Fundamentals

I'm going to use the example of basketball to illustrate my point, but the principles apply to every sport. Break the sport down to the simplest of terms—for instance, in individual offense: dribbling and ball handling, passing, shooting (post and perimeter), moves with and without the basketball, free throws, and so on. You, as the coach, should commit a certain amount of time every day to demonstrating the proper techniques of these fundamentals. Having your kids emulate these fundamentals correctly and making sure they realize why they're practicing them and how this relates to the overall game of basketball will be the ingredients to insure a successful season. If you do this with every aspect of the game, and remember, there are a lot of areas to cover (in any sport), your team will be confident and thoroughly prepared for the road ahead.

103

Conditioning

Coaches have widely divergent views on conditioning. Some coaches believe that any form of running that does not include a basketball is a waste of time. They will not even consider running a line drill without using a ball. I can understand this perspective but this way of thinking is short-sighted. I, too, like to involve balls in some of my conditioning. In fact, one of my favorite exercises is called the no dribble drill. Your team scrimmages full court without being allowed to dribble. This drill is wonderful for working on moving without the ball, passing, and making quick decisions on the run. The players love it and it is a great conditioner. However, I also take advantage of the conditioning portion of practice as a time to raise the level of fitness and mental toughness. This part of my practice which usually happens at the end is when I remind my team of our goals for the season and why we have to work so hard. It is not just wind sprints; it's running with a purpose.

It is a wonderful time to motivate your team. I believe you need to deserve success. By pushing yourself to the limit, by challenging yourself daily, by doing things you didn't think you could do, you are becoming stronger both physically and mentally. After a couple of weeks of this training, my players begin to feel as if they can accomplish anything. They take pride in how hard they work and they know that the success that they achieve is deserved. It is important to note that our entire practice is being done in this mind-set, not just the conditioning portion. We try to do everything at our highest level.

My teams have had a lot of success over the years. We have won many games and many championships. Nevertheless, whenever my former players get together to talk about their past experiences, they don't talk about how many games they won, they talk about how hard they worked and how much they loved it.

My all-time favorite Waldorf basketball quote came from one of my former players, Kris Seeley, who was being interviewed for a newspaper article after we defeated a big school. The writer asked Kris how he and his teammates could play so hard the entire game without any rest and very little substitution. Kris responded very matter-of-factly, "We get to rest on free throws." This is the Waldorf way. We know that we work harder than any other team. We even have shirts that say "nobody plays harder." My players know that I ask a lot from them and I think they would feel let down if I didn't. Remember: you need to deserve your success.

Conclusion

Throughout this book I have written about the wonderful benefits of team sports' bringing competition in a positive way, the vital role a coach plays, and how to build a successful program. Sports can play a big part in teaching children lifelong lessons. The way to really learn something is to be fully awake and alive and want to "drink" the information in. Sports gives kids this opportunity better than any other vehicle. Youngsters want and need to be passionate about something and sports are a great vessel for channeling those feelings. Remember, it's not the game. It's not the final score. It's kids learning values and virtues in a healthy environment, and applying them to all aspects of life. What more could you ask for?

Instill competition the right way. Teach your players the true meaning of the word. Competition is about playing to your best ability. It's a part of goal setting and evaluating your performance. It's a criterion to determine what is working and what needs improvement. Competition is not about the opponent. If your players understand this, they'll always appreciate and reach for the true nature of sport.

Take advantage of your position. You have the opportunity to play a vital role in children's lives. To me, there's nothing of greater importance in the world. You are helping to secure a better tomorrow. Prepare yourself, stand for and live by the virtues that you believe in, and teach with passion.

Finally, get your entire school involved—from the administration and faculty, to the student body and local community. Make your program one the whole school can be proud of.

I hope this book has shed some light on the subject of coaching and sports. It is my most sincere hope that you can put this book to use, that it can help start and/or improve your program, and help shape your own philosophies on coaching. My career has been incredibly rewarding. I wish you the same.

EPILOGUE—THE FUTURE

The future belongs to those who believe in the possibility of their dreams.

— Franklin D. Roosevelt

Substance abuse, domestic violence, strike, lock out, salary caps: these are the terms in the sports pages nowadays. Everywhere you turn, some big name athlete is being reprimanded, suspended, or even jailed for his outlandish behavior. Is this what sports has come to in today's society? Is this going to be the norm as we head into the 21st century?

Sports is entering a delicate time. Fans are becoming fed up with the high salary, low moral attitude of the players, the unsportsmanlike conduct of the coaches, and out-of-control greed of the owners. Every strike, hold out, drug bust, and so on is pushing the fans further and further away. So how can we turn this around? What is it going to take? To start the slow process of change, I believe you have to look to the coaches. Parents obviously play a very important role in instilling the proper morals and ethics in their children as they raise them, but it's up to the coaches to teach the children the true meaning of sport. If more coaches of tomorrow will appreciate the huge responsibility they have in shaping these young athletes and give them a positive role model to look up to, I think we will have fewer and fewer problems with the above mentioned behavior in the future.

And in conveying this meaning, coaches can instill lifelong lessons that athletes can apply in other areas of their life including health and fitness, academic endeavors, and career opportunities, to name a few. So coaches, the ball is in your court. You have the opportunity of a lifetime: the chance to make a difference in someone's life. Seize it.

107

POSTSCRIPT

When I finished writing the first edition of my book in '97, I felt I had put down on paper everything that I wanted to say. A couple of years later when it was up for a reprint, I realized there was more to add, partly because Waldorf teachers and coaches all over the country have called with comments, questions, and feedback from their experiences, and partly because of my continual search to learn, improve, and experience coaching to the fullest extent. A lot has happened in the last two years. I have stepped down from coaching baseball, my first true love, advanced to the section final four for a record ninth consecutive season in basketball, and experienced my first "losing" season (We didn't lose; we just ran out of time.) the following year. Yet, the one constant thing that has remained is my love for my players and my gratitude for being a part of the Waldorf community. You have blessed my life.

A Waves Athlete

You wonder why he does it
Striving to improve each and every day.
Look only to his work ethic
He knows no other way.

You wonder why he does it
It's all about being a Wave.
He has seen the players before him
And how their road was paved.

You wonder why he does it
Discipline and pride spells his name.
You wonder why he does it
He plays for the love of the game.

                                    Dean Stark

REFERENCES

Colgan, Michael, *The New Nutrition*. Vancouver, British Columbia: Apple Publishing, 1995.

Douillard, John, *Body, Mind and Spirit*. New York: Crown Trade Paperbacks, 1994.

Haas, Robert, *Eat to Win*. New York: Rawson Associates, 1993.

Kischnick, Rudolf, *Games, Gymnastics, and Sports in Child Development*. London: Rudolf Steiner Press, 1979.

Krause, Jerry, ed., *Coaching Basketball*. Chicago: NTC Contemporary Publishing Group, Inc., 1994.

Riley, Pat, *The Winner Within*. New York: G.P. Putnam and Sons, 1993.

Steiner, Rudolf, *Education for Adolescents*. Hudson, New York: Anthroposophic Press, 1921.

Wooden, John, *They Call Me Coach*. New York: Bantam Books, 1973.